HOTSPOTS
CRETE

Written by Brian and Eileen Anderson, updated by Andrew Sanger
Front cover photography courtesy of Thomas Cook Tour Operations Ltd

Original design concept by Studio 183 Limited
Series design by the Bridgewater Book Company
Cover design/artwork by Lee Biggadike, Studio 183 Limited

Produced by the Bridgewater Book Company
The Old Candlemakers, West Street, Lewes, East Sussex BN7 2NZ, United Kingdom
www.bridgewaterbooks.co.uk
Project Editor: Emily Casey Bailey
Project Designer: Lisa McCormick

Published by Thomas Cook Publishing
A division of Thomas Cook Tour Operations Limited
PO Box 227, Units 15-16, Coningsby Road, Peterborough PE3 8SB, United Kingdom
email: books@thomascook.com
www.thomascookpublishing.com
+ 44 (0) 1733 416477

ISBN-13: 978-1-84157-539-1
ISBN-10: 1-84157-539-9

First edition © 2006 Thomas Cook Publishing
Text © 2006 Thomas Cook Publishing
Maps © 2006 Thomas Cook Publishing
Head of Thomas Cook Publishing: Chris Young
Project Editor: Diane Ashmore
Production/DTP Editor: Steven Collins

Printed and bound in Spain by Graficas Cems, Navarra, Spain

CONTENTS

SYMBOLS KEY

The following is a key to the symbols used throughout this book:

i	information office	✉	post office	↘	tip
P	car park	✝	church	🛍	shopping
🚌	bus stop	🛡	police station	🍴	restaurant
🚻	WC	✈	airport	◉	fine dining
☎	telephone	🛒	supermarket	▣	cafe
✚	hospital				

---

① telephone   **⑦** fax   **ⓔ** email   **ⓦ** website address

ⓐ address   **ⓛ** opening times   **❶** important

€ budget price   €€ mid-range price   €€€ most expensive

★ specialist interest   ★★ see if passing   ★★★ top attraction

---

INTRODUCTION
Getting to know Crete

SEA OF CRETE

Rodopou
Peninsula

Afrata •

Kolymbari

MALEME

PLATNIAS

AGHIA MARINA

CHANIA ✈

KASTELLI

Spilia •

Episkopi •

RETHYMNON

Platanes

Omalos •

Mili •

Eleftherna •

Samaria Gorge

2453 m

Arkadi Monast

Xyloskalo •

Samaria •

Elafonissi

PALEOHORA

Sougia

AGHIA ROUMELI

HORA SFAKION

Spili •

PLAKIAS

2456

Aghios
Pavlos

AGHIA
GALINI

Aghia Triada •

Pitsidia •

LIBYAN SEA

Getting to know Crete

The largest and most southerly of all the Greek islands, Crete is barely more than a four-hour flight from most of Europe's capitals. It is a place to soak up the summer sun, learn to say avrio ('tomorrow'), discover a taste for raki and retsina and enjoy lazy days cooling in the sea.

GEOGRAPHY

Almost cigar-shaped, the island is 250 km (156 miles) long, but fairly narrow. It is the most southerly part of Europe and is just 300 km (187 miles) off the coast of Africa. The island is dominated by the huge backbone of the White Mountains (Levka Ori) in the west, the Mount Ida massif in the centre (this provides the highest peak – Psiloritis – at 2456 m, or over 8000 ft) and the Lasithi mountains towards the east. Gorges are a feature of these mountains, the most famous of these being the Samaria Gorge (see page 71).

LIFESTYLE

The Cretans are farmers and fishermen at heart. Olives and vines, both labour-intensive crops at certain times of the year, remain central to the economy, but figs, almonds, citrus fruits, apricots and melons are also grown and eaten, and form the basis of the 'Mediterranean diet', what scientists have recently called the healthiest in the developed world.

WILD FLOWERS

Summer visitors might find it hard to believe that Crete is a mass of flowers throughout the spring months. Autumn rains start the flowering season with the little white-flowered *Cyclamen creticum*, and a host of other bulbous plants, coming into bloom. The real riot of flowers does not arrive until around late March, when the anemones start to fill the olive groves. Wild orchids are something of a speciality, with more than 50 species to find, with names such as yellow bee orchid, naked man orchid and purple limodore. Another interesting plant to watch for is the big turban buttercup, which grows in white and yellow forms on Crete.

⬭ *Tzermiado, a traditional village on the Lasithi Plateau*

TRADITIONAL VILLAGES

It is very easy on Crete to slip off the mantle of tourism to find some
enchanting, unspoilt village and sit in the square shaded by an ancient
plane tree, just watching the world go by. One or two villages have
become particularly popular, including Kritsa, near Aghios Nikolaos
(see page 62): the fact that it is now a craft centre adds to its undoubted
charms. Mochos, on the way up to Lasithi (see page 81), is another village
with a good atmosphere.

The best of Crete

EARLY CIVILIZATIONS

Crete is widely recognized as the cradle of European civilization. The Minoans can be traced back more than 4000 years and they left behind a remarkable number of palace sites and towns, which are spread all around the island. Later inhabitants, too, left more than footprints.

- **Knossos**, without doubt the island's top site, provides a deep insight into an ancient way of life (see page 77).
- **Faistos** (see page 74) is a huge Minoan palace site, beautifully located with plenty to see.
- **Gortys** (see page 74) is an important Roman capital city.
- **Lato**, an ancient Greek city state, high in the mountains, is not only spectacular, but also free.
- **Gournia**, you can walk the narrow streets of an ancient Minoan town, inspect the living areas and admire the location.

LASITHI PLATEAU

High in the middle of the Lasithi mountains lies a fertile plateau that has been farmed for thousands of years and still provides a unique lifestyle (see page 81). Once dotted with as many as 10,000 windmills all busy raising irrigation water, only a fraction remain today. Photographic opportunities abound and you might even capture one of the traditional images of Greece: an old lady in black riding on a donkey.

SAMARIA GORGE

Europe's most famous and spectacular gorge (see page 71) can only be explored on foot. A certain fitness is required, but tired muscles for the next couple of days provide the perfect excuse not to leave the sun-lounger! There are no trophies, just a huge sense of achievement.

RESORTS
Places under the sun

Chania
Crete's prettiest port

The focal point for exploration in charming Chania (pronounced 'Han-ya') is the elegant Venetian harbour, with its colour-washed facades and buzzing café atmosphere. The town is also renowned for its atmospheric old quarter, fort and museums. You can shop for souvenirs in the narrow streets behind the harbour, and seek out the famous Leather Alley – or inspect the delicious local produce on sale in the bustling covered market.

Chania's Venetian harbour front is ringed by cafés, bars and restaurants, behind which runs Zambeliou, the street that leads into the heart of the old quarter. Search here for souvenirs, or lunch in one of the atmospheric tavernas, found among the tangle of narrow alleyways. Alternatively, snack on fresh bread or a *tiropitta* (small pastry filled with cheese) from the wood burning *fournos* (bakery) on Theotokopoulou. Firkas Fort and the Naval Museum (see page 14) stand guard at the western end of the harbour, while Kastelli, at the eastern end, is the site of the earliest settlement in Chania. Below Kastelli hill, the domes of the Mosque of the Janissaries form a feature at the harbour edge. Walk around the mosque to the inner harbour to view the remains of the Venetian Arsenali (dry docks). Continue past the harbour to the lighthouse, past the *fortezza* (the old fortifications, now a restaurant), for good views over the town.

 Tourist information in Chania
Greek tourist office ⓐ Kriari 40, by 1866 Square ⓣ 28210 92943
ⓞ Open Mon–Fri 07.30–14.30
Chania information office ⓐ Kydonias 29 ⓣ 28210 36155
ⓔ chania@ofcrete.gr ⓦ www.chania.gr

◑ *Courtyard in Chania's old town*

THINGS TO SEE & DO

Archaeological Museum ★★★

The former Venetian Church of San Francesco, once the island's grandest building, makes an ideal setting for Minoan storage jars, wonderfully decorated clay coffins, sculptures, glassware and mosaics from Greek and Roman times. ⓐ 21 Odos Chalidon ⓣ 28210 90334 ⓛ Open Tues–Sun 08.30–15.00, closed Mon ⓘ Admission charge

Boat trips ★★

Boat trips include excursions to the island of Theodorou, home of the native wild goat and ancient city of Akitos. Other boats go to Doru, Theo and the Lazaretta islands. Try the glass-bottomed boat for unforgettable views of the seabed and the wreckage of a World War II aeroplane.

Cretan House Folklore Museum ★★

A working museum where the equipment for traditional crafts is on display and also in use. Local embroidery and tapestries are on sale. ⓐ Odos Chalidon (signposted down an alley near the Archaeological Museum) ⓣ 28210 90816 ⓛ Open Mon–Fri 09.30–15.00 and 18.00–21.00, Sat and Sun 09.00–14.00 ⓘ Admission charge

Diving ★★

Divers can discover a Chania as beautiful below the water as it is above. One of many diving centres, **Blue Adventures Diving**, caters for all abilities. ⓐ Venetian harbour ⓣ 28210 40608 ⓦ www.blueadventuresdiving.gr

Firkas Fort and Naval Museum ★★

Wander freely around Firkas Fort before visiting the museum. Inside is a superb model of old Chania, detailed models of boats through the ages and a poignant exhibition of the Battle of Crete (1941). Children will love the mock-up of a battleship operations room. ⓛ Open 10.00–14.00, closed public holidays ⓘ Free admission for children up to 12; senior citizen and student discounts

Those arriving by car will find easy, convenient and free parking along the seafront, by the city walls on the western side, behind Firkas Fort. Beware of parking elsewhere as the fines can be expensive.

Limnoupolis Water Park ★★

Plenty of fun here to keep the family entertained, from water-slides and swimming pools to the climbing wall, playgrounds, shops and restaurants.
ⓐ 8 km (5 miles) west of Chania on the road to Omalos ☎ 28210 33246
ⓦ www.limnoupolis.gr ⏰ Open daily in season 10.00–19.00
❶ Admission charge; Visa and MasterCard accepted

Horse and carriage rides ★★

Drive around Chania in style. The starting point is from beside the Mosque of the Janissaries.

The Little Train ★★

This lovely 20-minute journey around old Chania leaves every half-hour from beside the Firkas Fort on the western side of the town.
☎ 28210 68782 ⏰ Open 08.00–21.00 ❶ Small charge

⬤ *Fish restaurants line Chania's harbour*

RESTAURANTS

The harbourside restaurants have the best views and atmosphere, especially after dark when the harbour lights are reflected in the water. Scenery comes at a price, however, and you can avoid the harbour area's high prices by choosing a café or taverna in the streets of the old town behind. Head beyond the Arsenali to the far end of the inner harbour for the best of the fish tavernas.

Amphora €€ ❶ The best of the restaurants on the quayside, this quiet, well-run establishment specializes in traditional Cretan dishes like *boureki* (courgette, cheese and potato bake) and *kalitsounia* (sweetened cheese pastry), all deliciously prepared and attractively presented. ❸ Quayside ❶ 28210 93224 ❶ Open 11.30–midnight, closed Oct–Apr ❶ Amex, Visa and MasterCard accepted

Fortezza €€€ ❷ Restaurants do not come much more romantic than this one. It is set in the sea wall next to the lighthouse. A free ferry shuttles people across from the harbour, otherwise it would be a

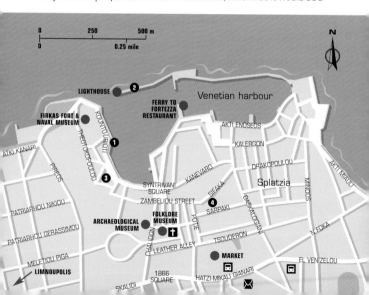

long walk round. They serve an international cuisine that is a bit pricey but worth the expense for a special occasion. ⓐ Venetian harbour ❶ 28210 46546/55649 ❶ Visa and MasterCard accepted

Tamam €€ ❸ Housed in an atmospheric former Turkish bath inside a 16th-century building in the heart of the old quarter, this excellent taverna is always busy. Make sure you get there early, or be prepared to wait. ⓐ 49 Zambeliou Street ❶ 28210 96080 ⓛ Open all day past midnight

Well of the Turk €€ ❹ This is a difficult restaurant to find, tucked away in a mass of lanes in the old Splantzia district. Try and make the effort, because it is a delightful place away from the busy port. Ask to see the well. They serve good Middle Eastern, Cretan and Greek food. ⓐ 1–3 Kalinikou Sarpaki, Splanzia ❶ 28210 54547 ⓛ Open Wed–Sun 19.30–late, closed Mon and Tues

BEACHES

The nearest beach, **Nea Hora**, is a short walk beyond Firkas Fort, and has cafés and restaurants.

NIGHTLIFE

There are many good bars and nightclubs around Chania's old quarter. Try **El Mundo** and **Point** music bars, or **Klik**, the Scandinavian disco at the Venetian harbour for an all-night dance and party atmosphere.

Aghia Marina & Platanias
the ideal get-away-from-it-all resorts

Just west of Chania lies a string of idyllic resorts where the pace of life is anything but stressful. It starts with Aghia Marina, a friendly resort blessed with one of the best beaches in the area. Aghia Marina seems to run into Platanias, and the two could almost be classed as one long resort, but Platanias is the more lively of the two and this is where you will find most of the shops and restaurants.

The whole coastline here has a good selection of beaches and all are conveniently connected to one another by a busy coast road. Shops, restaurants, and a wealth of things to see and do make this an area people return to each year.

 As this is such a long resort, it is a good idea to rent a bicycle. It is also convenient, due to lack of car parking space in the resort.

⬤ *View of Aghia Marina from Stalos*

THINGS TO SEE & DO
Cycle in the hills ★★

There are several bike-hire shops in the resort, from where the adventurous can explore the steep little lanes among the olive groves that rise on the hills behind the resorts. In just minutes, you have fabulous views out to sea and along the coast well beyond the city of Chania.

Active excursions ★★

Treks on foot or by mountain bike, as well as kayaking, rapelling, canyoning and more are organized by **Trekking Plan**. They also take groups on walks down the Imbros Gorge, south of Chania. ⓐ Beside the Santa Marina Hotel ⓣ 28210 60861 ⓦ www.cycling.gr

Smile Park ★

This is a good place to take children. It is not a huge area, but it will keep them amused, playing on the bouncy castle, slides, and swings or testing their driving skills on the go-kart track. There are tables and chairs for the adults to relax and keep an eye on the fun. ⓐ On the border between Aghia Marina and Platanias ⓣ 28210 60700 ⓛ Open 17.00–dusk ⓘ Entry is free but there is a small charge for the rides

EXCURSIONS
The German War Cemetery ★★★

Hill 107 is where the German invasion began on 20 May 1941. More than 15,000 German soldiers lost their lives on Crete during the war and as many as 4500 here at Maleme. They are remembered with lines of flat headstones, each a double grave. ⓐ At Maleme, a few kilometres from Platanias ⓛ Open daily ⓘ Admission free

Kolymbari ★★

About 5 km (3 miles) from Maleme is the traditional fishing village of Kolymbari. Many visitors stop here to sample the fresh fish served in one of the numerous little restaurants and tavernas. There is no sandy beach here, but the water is clear and very tempting.

DRIVING EXCURSION

The drive on to the Rodopou peninsula up from Kolymbari is well worth it for the views back along the rocky coastline with Chania in the distance. The road loops back upon itself. Halfway along is the tiny town of Afrata, where you will find a few simple tavernas as well as a road that leads to a secret rocky cove.

The road south from Kolymbari climbs up towards Episkopi, where there are two unique churches. Past the town of Spilia is a sign on the right, pointing to the Chapel of Aghios Stefanos, a tiny 10th-century white-walled building sheltering below oak trees. The key should be in the door – inside, the chapel's walls are decorated with beautiful frescos.

Further on from here, and signposted, is the much larger Church of Mihail Arhangelos Episkopi, one of the oldest churches in Greece, with a unique dome. It has been suggested that the centre rotunda dates back to the first Byzantine period in the 6th century. The church is not always open but a guardian monk lives on site and you may be able to find him and ask to see the impressive frescos inside dating back to the 10th century.

BEACHES

Aghia Marina and Platanias are the focal points of a continuous development west of Chania that follows the coast road around a beautiful bay edged with sand-and-shingle beach most of the way.

Aghia Marina itself lies about 9 km (6 miles) from Chania, and has one of the best stretches of sand, with bars, tavernas, nightlife, low-rise accommodation and sports hire facilities right behind the beach. Some 3 km (2 miles) further along the coast road, livelier Platanias has a less-sandy beach.

RESTAURANTS

Drakiana € Away from the crowds, this ever-popular taverna under the trees is hidden away on a track through olive groves. Cretan cooking is a speciality, but with a range of other dishes.
📍 3 km (2 miles) off the main road, Platanias 📞 28210 61677

Maria's Restaurant €€ This popular and friendly taverna, with tables on an open-air terrace, offers a wide range of familiar Greek and Western-style dishes, but also has a good choice of traditional Cretan specialities. ➋ On the main road at Kato Stalos (the small resort on the Chania side of Aghia Marina) ➊ 28210 60119

Mylos €€€ This must be one of the best restaurants on the western Crete coastline. Perfect for that special occasion, the staff will go out of their way to make it memorable, organizing special requests like flowers, champagne and the like. Mylos was converted from a 14th-century watermill, and is tastefully decorated in traditional village style, complete with trees, herbs and a pond with its own ducks. ➋ On the main road in Platanias ➊ 28210 68578 ➍ Open 18.00–late ➊ All credit cards except Diners accepted

Old Village Restaurant € Situated at the top of Platanias' picturesque older village, this traditional taverna has fantastic views of the two resorts. ➋ Ano Platanias, on the hillside behind Platanias ➊ 28210 60119

NIGHTLIFE

There is a nightly exodus from Aghia Marina and Platanias, as many tourists and locals head into Chania for a quayside stroll, a leisurely meal in the old town and maybe an after-dinner drink in one of the open-air bars.

Later in the evening, tourists and locals alike flood back to Aghia Marina and Platanias for music and dancing at late-night bars and clubs along the main road. The clubs come and go every few months. A few that have survived several seasons are **Utopia**, **Mylos Club**, **Rock House** and, on the highway beyond Platanias, the more exclusive **Privilege**. Most of the area's nightclubs do not get going until after 23.00, and start to hot up after 01.00.

Rethymnon
fine fortress and bustling bazaar

Stealing all the attention in the vibrant resort of Rethymnon is the old Venetian town that lies at its heart. A maze of narrow alleyways, with a fascinating blend of Venetian and Turkish architecture, an atmospheric harbour and a huge Venetian fortress all combine in a relatively small area to make this one of the most interesting towns on Crete.

Seductive by night, Venetian facades and bustling tavernas line the intimate fishing harbour. Close by, up on the hill above the harbour, are the imposing Venetian fortress and the Archaeological Museum, watching over the narrow streets of the old town, with their fascinating choice of shops, cafés and tavernas.

Just 5 km (3 miles) from Rethymnon is Platanes (not to be confused with the town of Platanias near Aghia Marina), a perfect base for many of the area's main attractions. For a small town, it has a fair share of restaurants, bars and nightlife. The main beach road allows good access to both east and west coastlines.

THINGS TO SEE & DO
Archaeological Museum ★★
Built by the Turks as an extra defence for the fort entrance, the building later became a prison, before being converted into a museum. It has a small but interesting collection of local Minoan, Greek and Roman finds. The Minoan statuary and painted clay coffins are particularly worth a look, as is the Roman jewellery. ⓐ Opposite the fortress entrance
🕒 Open Tues–Sun 08.30–15.00, closed Mon ⓘ Admission charge

Boat trips ★★
Full-day trips and mini-cruises are on offer from **Dolphin Cruises**. The *Barbarosa* makes a daily trip from Rethymnon along the western coastline to Marathi. En route it stops so you can swim, and you may see dolphins. There are also two mini-cruises that operate daily.

The 'Captain Hook pirate ship' cruise sails east along the coast to the caves at Skaleta and the Camarola Arch, returning via the Fortezza. The other cruise goes via the caves, but stops at the fishing village of Panormos for an hour, where you can eat or enjoy a cooling dip in the sea. ⓐ Sailing from the Venetian harbour ⓣ 28310 57666

Historical and Folk Art Museum ★★
Recently resided in a 17th-century mansion, this is one for all the family – a fascinating collection of implements connected with traditional crafts, household goods, costumes and jewellery. It shows how everyday life changed very little in the centuries from the time of Venetian rule until relatively recently. ⓐ Odos Vernardou ⓣ 28310 23398 ⓛ Open Mon–Sat 10.00–14.00, closed Sun ⓘ Admission charge

Kart Club ★
There is a 600 m (1969 ft) track for modern 200cc karts. ⓐ On the coast road ⓣ 28310 71037

The Loggia ★★

This building is one of the most brilliant examples of Renaissance architecture in Crete. Originally used by the Venetian public authorities, it also served as a meeting place for the city's nobility. It is now an upmarket art shop. ➌ On the corner of Arkadidou and Paleologou 2

 Do not swim when the red flag is flying. The beach here has very strong undercurrents and each year, people die in these waters.

Diving ★★

Several diving companies based in town offer diving options, including PADI courses at **Paradise Dive Centre** ➋ 73 Venizelou ➊ 28310 53258

Mini-Train ★★

➋ Starts from Iroon Square and makes a circuit round town. ➌ Every half-hour, 10.00–23.00 ➊ Half-price for 3- to 12-year-olds

Porta Guora (Old Town Gate) ★

The only surviving gate of the ancient city walls. The nearby Public Gardens host a lively wine festival in the last two weeks of July.

Rimondi Fountain ★★

Three lions' heads spout water from this ancient fountain, the focal point of life in the old quarter.

The Venetian Fortress ★★★

Possibly the largest castle ever built, this was put up in the 16th century to repel pirate raids. There are splendid views from the ramparts, and a spacious interior with several buildings inside. ➊ 28310 28101 ➌ Open Tues–Sun 08.00–19.00, last entry 18.15, closed Mon ➊ Admission charge

Walking ★★★

The Happy Walker, a local company, offers six different walks, one for each day of the week (not Sunday) that range from pretty villages to

imposing gorges. **ⓐ** 56 Tobazi Street **ⓣ** 28310 52920
ⓔ www.happywalker.com **ⓛ** Open Apr–Oct 17.00–20.30

BEACHES

The town centre fronts directly onto a sandy beach with reasonable facilities, though it is sometimes crowded and dirty. For cleaner stretches, head eastwards from the town centre for around 6 km (nearly 4 miles). There is no shortage of sunbeds and umbrellas and there is a full range of water-based activities.

EXCURSIONS

Argyropouli ★★

This is a tranquil town, to the west of Rethymnon, with freshwater springs that are the source of water for the area. A good place for lunch and a refreshing drink.

⏷ *Bustling tavernas line the intimate harbour at Rethymnon*

Arkadi Monastery ★★★

This old, fort-like monastery, its history tied up with the Cretan struggle for independence, enjoys a great location in the hills. If driving, be sure to return via the characterful villages of Eleftherna and Margarites. ◐ Open 08.00–20.00, closes for lunch 13.00–15.30 ❶ Small admission fee

Mili ★★

Five kilometres (3 miles) east of Rethymnon there is a turning to this deserted pretty village that is well worth a visit.

 Persuasive timeshare touts operate in Platanes and Rethymnon. Do not make any decisions you may later regret.

RESTAURANTS (see map on page 23)

Avli Restaurant €€€ ❶ Eat inside, underneath curved cellar walls or outside in the pretty courtyard for a memorable meal. Once a 17th-century Venetian manor house, it now serves Cretan *mezedes*, small bites of food similar to Spanish *tapas*. Try the local wild goat cooked in thyme and honey, or pick a speciality from the 'creative cooking' heading in the menu. ⓐ 22 Xanthoulidou ❶ 28310 26213 ◐ Open noon–late ❶ All credit cards accepted

La Crêperie € ❷ Within sight of the Rimondi fountain, this cheap fast food restaurant offers good-quality sweet and savoury pancakes. See the daily specials board. You can sit inside or opt for a takeaway. ⓐ 10 Arabatzoglou Street, in the old quarter ❶ 28310 50230

Lemonokipos €€ ❸ Tables here are set under fragrant lemon trees in an old-quarter courtyard; its varied menu has good Cretan specialities. ⓐ 100 Andistasis ❶ 28310 57087 ❶ Credit cards accepted

Maria's Taverna € ❹ A friendly, popular and traditional taverna, with outdoor tables under a leafy awning, and dessert and raki

ARCHELON – THE SEA TURTLE PROTECTION SOCIETY
This group has a harbourfront booth to promote awareness of loggerhead turtles that lay their eggs on some of Crete's beaches during June and August. ☎ 28310 72288 ✉ www.archelon.gr

on the house. ⓐ 20 Moshovitou, on a side street near the Rimondi Fountain ☎ 28310 29078 🕐 Open all evening ❶ Cards accepted

Samaria € ❺ One of the best of the seafront tavernas, with tables outdoors and an array of tasty meat dishes. ⓐ Venizelou ☎ 28310 24681 ❶ Credit cards accepted

Veneto Restaurant €€ ❻ Spectacularly set in a small back alley in a former 14th-century monastery and a later 16th century Venetian palace, the inside is stunning, as is the tempting, secluded courtyard around the back. ⓐ 4 Epimenidou ☎ 28310 56634 🕐 Open 09.00–late ❶ Visa and MasterCard accepted

RESTAURANTS IN PLATANES

Kellari Restaurant €€ This restaurant has a huge menu and regular Cretan special. ⓐ 153 Mahis Kritis, on main road opposite supermarket ☎ 28310 51882 🕐 Open 10.00–midnight ❶ Cards accepted

Zisi €€ The place for a traditional Greek menu. Choose your food from a display behind the glass counter. ⓐ Between Platanes and Rethymnon ☎ 28310 28814 🕐 Open noon–01.00

NIGHTLIFE

Nightlife revolves around the streets of the old quarter, the Venetian harbour and the seafront road. The road between the harbour and Iroon Square is closed to traffic every evening. Try the **Rock Café**, **Fortezza** and **NYC-Metropolis**. For drinks and chat, try the **Punch Bowl Irish Bar**.

Aghia Galini
friendly harbour town

Squeezed in on three sides by a huge mountain range at the foot of the Amari Valley, Aghia Galini has grown up from a remote fishing village into a popular resort.

The narrow streets are lined with white houses and the usual restaurants and tavernas. The buildings appear stacked on top of each other, set into the pretty hillside. The three main streets lead to the harbour, where you will find fishing boats and daily cruises to nearby attractions.

THINGS TO SEE & DO
Cruises ★
There are daily cruises to many nearby islands and beaches, and some are well worth the trip. Paximadia Island, 12 km (7.5 miles) offshore, is one place you might want to visit for its lovely sandy beaches.

Fishing ★
Trips can be arranged from the harbour. One boat advertises that they will cook whatever you catch and also supplies wine.

Fishing is good this side of the island – if you are keen to catch a fish, you can buy a cheap rod and tackle. Otherwise, there are boat excursions that offer the loan of a rod as part of their package.

EXCURSIONS
Aghios Georgios ★★
It is possible to walk to this shingle cove, but the boat will be much easier. It is a great place to relax and take an easy lunch at one of the two tavernas. Water taxis are available from the harbour.

◀ *The pretty hillside town of Aghia Galini*

Aghios Pavlos ★★

Further away than Aghios Georgios and more attractive with its
sheltered bay, impressive rock formations and good snorkelling.
There is another beach near here that can be reached by walking
west over the headland. Water taxis are available from the harbour.

Plakias ★★

This town, 30 km (19 miles) to the west, is similar to Aghia Galini, but
perhaps a better base for exploring the countryside and nearby beaches.
It also has the Kourtaliotiko Gorge, famous for its stunning scenery and
rare wildlife.

BEACHES

To the east of Aghia Galini are a few narrow bays where you can
sunbathe and swim in the clear water. There are parasols and sunbeds
for hire. On the gravelled path to the sea there is a water sports centre.
The beach is also lined with tavernas.

RESTAURANTS

There are no road names, but all the following restaurants are easy
enough to find.

Madame Hortense €€ A rooftop restaurant, slightly to one side
of the hub of the other tavernas. The tasteful decoration is
enhanced by the vine winding its way along the balcony. Excellent
Mediterranean specialities such as *poulet à la cubaine*, chicken fillet
served with a sauce of seasonal fruits. ☎ 28320 91215 ⏰ Open 18.00–late
ⓘ Visa and MasterCard accepted

Onar €€ Most restaurants in the town have great views over
the harbour, but this must be one of the best. From under awnings
on the second floor you can see most of the town. Good Greek menu;
the barracuda fillet is tempting, if a little pricey. ☎ 28320 91288
⏰ Open 11.00–late ⓘ Visa and MasterCard accepted

🔺 *The town of Aghia Galini rises up from the harbour*

🍴 **Zefyros** €€ This pleasant restaurant has an informative menu with detailed explanations of each dish. It is a large, clean place with crisp blue-and-white tablecloths. The chicken on the spit is a speciality. ❸ On the harbourfront ❶ 28320 91290 🕒 Open 10.00–late ❶ Visa and MasterCard accepted

NIGHTLIFE

There are loads of bars and the odd disco down around the bottom of Taverna street and the harbour. **Paradiso** and **Zorba's** are the most popular.

Matala
old hippie haunt

The honey-coloured cliffs, dotted with caves that overlook a long curvaceous beach, have made this town famous.

These Roman or early Christian burial tombs were hippie hang-outs in the 1960s. Famous names such as Cat Stevens and Bob Dylan are said to have lived in the caves, taking advantage of the free shelter. Matala is now a busy resort, attracting tourists by the busload. It is only a small town and visitors mainly come here to hang out on the beautiful sandy beach. A single main road leads into the resort, then curves around into the old town, which is packed with souvenir shops, food stalls, currency exchanges and travel agents. Even though Matala can get busy during the early afternoon, if you get here in the morning or wait until the crowds have gone, you will find it magical to stare out towards the caves, watching the sun set, armed with your favourite cocktail.

There's a large car park as you enter Matala, but further into town you'll find sheltered parking with an attendant. It is clearly signposted to the left and well worth the small charge.

THINGS TO SEE & DO
The caves ★★★
The caves are now fenced off and there is a small charge to wander around the fascinating cliffs. In the evening the place is locked up and patrolled by security guards to discourage people from having parties here. The caves are well worth looking around for their elaborate decor. Inside are carved windows, seats and benches. During World War II, the caves doubled as munitions dumps, and then in the 1960s a large foreign community gathered here.

◀ *Fascinating cliffs and caves overlook the beach at Matala*

Melanouri Horse Farm ★★

On the main road into Matala is the village of Pitsidia, where this ranch
is situated. There are organized rides for all abilities of horsemanship.
The trip through the olive groves to neighbouring villages sounds
marvellous, as does the sunset ride on Como beach. A picnic of olives,
bread, cheeses and wine is provided. ☎ 28920 45040
ⓦ www.melanouri.com ⓔ info@melanouri.com

Sunset

A very enjoyable way to spend your time in Matala is to find a central
position above the horseshoe-shaped bay in the late afternoon and wait
for the sunset; said to be among the most spectacular on the island.

BEACHES

The main beach below the caves is the centre of attraction for visitors
to Matala. The swimming here is very good, if a little rough at times.
The rocks by the caves make a convenient platform for divers. Snorkelling
is also popular because the water is filled with a variety of brightly
coloured fish. Every facility is provided – showers, toilets, changing
rooms, parasols – and at the back of the beach there are trees that
provide some excellent shelter from the sun.

◑ *Rock-cut tombs at Matala*

Sometimes the beach does get very crowded and if it is too much then you could head south, climbing over the cliffs behind the town to Red Beach. It is only a 20-minute walk away and well worth it for its dark-red, coloured sand. Be aware that this beach is a renowned nudist haunt.

RESTAURANTS

Corali € This restaurant offers breakfast and a good selection of steaks, grills and Greek specialities. There is not much seafood on the menu, so you might want to consider another restaurant if you like fish. ⓐ Away from the beach in a pleasant square behind the main throng of shops ☎ 28920 45744 🕑 Open 08.00–late

Skala € This small, family-run restaurant, serves traditional Greek food, away from the hordes of other places hogging the beach. It is a very cosy place and it has the most fantastic views to the cliffs and caves. Mrs Marina does all the cooking and her daughter helps out in the restaurant. The fish is always fresh and the special Cretan salad is highly recommended. ⓐ A short walk south around the bay, through a bar and up some uneven steps ☎ 28920 45489 🕑 Open 09.00–late ❶ Cash only

Waves € A reasonably priced restaurant overlooking the beach, serving fish and meat that is all cooked on the barbecue. Try *à la chef* – chicken served with a mushroom, paprika and cream sauce. ☎ 28920 45361 🕑 Open 09.30–late ❶ Visa and MasterCard accepted

EXCURSIONS

The town of Pitsidia is worth a visit not just because of the horse farm but also because it is quieter than Matala. To the north is Kalamaki, a long, empty beach with a few places to eat. Kommos, which lies just south of Kalamaki, is another option. It is an important archaeological site, being a Minoan harbour town. The site is not officially open yet as they are still excavating, but that does not mean you cannot take a look at what they are working on.

Iraklion
capital of Crete

Your first taste of present-day Iraklion, the fifth largest city in Greece, will give you little idea of the treasures behind its ancient walls. Dusty, bustling and noisy, Iraklion is easy to dislike, but hidden within a relatively compact area you will find some of the best shopping around, a lively street market, cafés set in leafy squares and one of the most important collections of archaeological finds in all of Greece. Children, especially, will love the castle down by the tranquil marina.

Start a tour of the sights at the small fishing harbour/marina, alongside the Venetian Arsenali, the dry docks where ships were once overhauled and built. Visit the Venetian Fort (see page 39), before heading up 25 Avgoustou Street into the city centre. (A short diversion from here leads to the Historical Museum of Crete – see page 38). Please note that 25 Avgoustou (the main road from port to town) is closed to cars at certain times of day (see tips box, page 38).

Watch out for Aghios Titos Church, set back in the square on the left. Built during the Byzantine era, then rebuilt by the Venetians, it served time as a Turkish mosque before being converted back to Christian use in 1925. Its prize possession is a reliquary containing the skull of St Titos, an important saint on the island. The shaded café here makes an inviting coffee stop.

A classic arcade announces the Loggia (Town Hall), once a meeting-place for Venetian nobility, before you pass Aghios Markos Church and enter the bustling hub of Platia el Venizelou (Venizelou Square), with its outdoor cafés and Morosini Fountain. The structure was named after Morosini, who was governor in 1627 when it was built, but the lions are on the fountain predate the rest of it by a few hundred years.

The lively, pedestrianized Odos 1866 street, home to the Saturday morning market, leads to Kornarou Square, with a Turkish pumphouse, now a café, and the Bembo Fountain. Turn right here, then round and

⬤ *The Venetian Fort at Iraklion*

down Loukareos to the Cathedral of St Minas. Pass to the left and along-side the older Church of St Caterina behind the cathedral.

Clothes shops begin to feature more strongly now as the route meets Odos 1821 and goes left back to Platia el Venizelou. Shopaholics might fancy a foray along Dikeossinis. The main route continues right into Dedalou, opposite the Morosini Fountain, a Mecca for serious shoppers.

Emerge into the expanse of Platia Eleftherias, where the large yellow building to the left houses Iraklion's Archaeological Museum, which specializes in Minoan artefacts (see next page).

25 Avgoustou Street (the main road from port to town) is closed to cars between 09.00–14.00 and 18.00–21.00. Follow signs off the main road to the port and park along the roadside before the bus station, which is on the left just beyond the port. There is a charge for car parking in this area.

THINGS TO SEE & DO

Archaeological Museum ★★★

The museum houses the most important collection of Minoan finds anywhere in the world. A visit to this museum will enhance excursions to Knossos and other sites on the island. There are plenty of artefacts to give a good insight into the everyday life of the Minoans, with explanations in English. There are also Greek and Roman finds on display. ⓐ Eleftherias Square ❶ 2810 226092 ❶ Open Tues–Sun 08.00–19.00, Mon 12.30–19.00 ❶ Admission charge

Churches ★★

The Cathedral of St Minas is a very impressive 19th-century building dominating St Catherine's Square. Just beside it stands the original, medieval St Minas Church. But much more interesting is Aghia Ekaterini (Church of St Caterina), just at the bottom of the same square. It is not only a church but also a **Museum of Religious Art**, housing a fine collection of Cretan icons. ⓐ St Catherine's Square ❶ Open Mon–Sat 10.00–13.00, Tues, Thurs and Fri 16.00–18.00 ❶ Small admission charge

Historical Museum ★★

A must for museum buffs, this museum provides the opportunity to view artefacts from the Byzantine, Venetian and Turkish periods. Also housed in the museum is the library and study of Nikos Kazantzakis, author of *Zorba the Greek*, as well as relics of the Battle of Crete, a selection of folk art and a re-creation of the interior of a Cretan farmhouse. ⓐ 7 Kalokairinou St ❶ 2810 283219 ❶ Open Mon–Fri 09.00–17.00, Sat 09.00–14.00, closed Sun ❶ Admission charge

Elegant shops line the streets of Dikeossinis and Dedalou (near the Morosini fountain), and the shops around Odos 1821 and Platia el Venizelou are worth a look. There is a huge Saturday market by the bus station near the city's port.

Kulés (Venetian Fort) ★★★

Superb views can be had from the ramparts of the renovated 16th-century Rocca al Mare, still known by its Turkish name of Kúles. The internal rooms are intact and a few cannons and a collection of cannon balls lie scattered around to add to the atmosphere.

❸ Venetian harbour 🕒 Open Mon–Sat 08.00–18.00, Sun 10.00–15.00

ⓘ Admission charge

EXCURSION

Fodele ★★

Time permitting, there is a short detour from Iraklion to this near by village and beach. Most people visit Fodele because it is claimed by some as the birthplace of Crete's most famous artist, El Greco. Not that it should be the sole reason for visiting this very pretty town that lies 3 km (2 miles) inland from the main road. It is also a good place to buy handmade local embroidery or to just relax in a shady café, drinking a glass of freshly squeezed orange juice.

To the right of the main road is Fodele's beach, a large sandy cove with all facilities. The beach is flanked on both sides by mountains. If you eat in the tavernas of Zorbas or Plaitis you are entitled to use their sunbeds and loungers free of charge.

A water sports provider operates from the back of a German truck that is located at the far west of the beach. El Greco's house and museum are located next to the charming Church of Panayia.

El Greco's house The famous artist's house is not in the town's main square, but is found by crossing a bridge on the right as you enter Fodele town. This well-signposted route heads north past orange groves.

The Church of Panayia On the way to the house and museum is the 14th-century Church of Panayia, which was built over an 8th-century basilica. The inside of the church contains outstanding 13th- and 14th-century frescos 🕐 Open 09.00–17.00, closed Mon
ⓘ Small admission charge

El Greco Museum This museum pays homage to the 16th-century painter whose religious paintings found great favour in Venice.
ⓘ 2810 521500 🕐 Open 09.00–17.00, closed Mon (The café next door is open the same times as the museum) ⓘ Small admission charge

RESTAURANTS (see map opposite)
Crete's capital has a wide choice of places to eat and an abundance of pavement cafés/restaurants.

🔲 **Chicken Souvláki** € ❶ Do not go looking for the name printed here since this is a translation from the Greek. Perfect for a quick snack, with some of the best kebabs in Crete. Watch what the locals are ordering and copy them. ❸ On a busy corner right next door to the Loggia (Town Hall) 🕐 Open 09.00–very late

🔲 **Giakoumis** € ❷ This unassuming place is easy to miss because it is in a tiny covered alley off the main market, among other similar-looking cafés. Ask for directions because it is worth hunting down. All the cooking is done over a hot grill; veal, steaks, pork, lamb chops and the best meatballs in the whole of Crete. ❸ Fot. Theodasaki 5–8 Str. ⓘ 2810 280277/ 284039 🕐 Open 07.00–22.00, closed Sun
ⓘ Visa and MasterCard accepted

Luculos €€€ ❸ This is a very upmarket restaurant situated in a quiet, pretty street. Diners have the choice of eating outside in the courtyard, which is dotted with atmospheric lime trees, or trying inside with its wooden panelling and starched white linen tablecloths. The staff are more friendly than you might expect in a restaurant with the reputation of being the best in town. The menu is international. This is certainly a great place to impress.
ⓐ 5 Korai ❶ 2810 224435 ● Open noon–01.00 ❶ All major credit cards accepted

Terzakis €€ ❹ This restaurant is minutes from the port and if you arrive in Iraklion at lunchtime, this is a good place to eat and plan where you want to go after lunch. Set in a quiet alley with a laid-back atmosphere. Serves excellent Greek food and very fresh fish, probably due to its close proximity to the port.
ⓐ 17 Manneli ❶ 2810 221444 ● Open 12 30–00.30 ❶ All major credit cards accepted

NIGHTLIFE

The best bars are in Platia Korai, a pleasant square behind Dedalou. Or you could try the more touristy area around Platia el Venizelou. Most young Iraklions seem to be content to watch the world go by from these bars and cafés, chatting with their friends. Backgammon is a very lively pursuit in Crete and everyone seems to be playing it. There are not many nightclubs in the city centre, but there are plenty of bars with loud music. Just follow the crowds and you will rarely go wrong.

Parking is notoriously difficult in Iraklion. From the main road follow the signs to the port. Just past here is a roundabout; turn right and you can park, for a charge, anywhere in this area.

● *Iraklion harbour*

Kokkini Hani
good beach resort

Handily situated for Iraklion, Kokkini Hani (also known as Hani Kokkini) is a small resort bypassed by the new Iraklion road and located in a quiet backwater on the old road. It looks on to a long, narrow stretch of sandy beach, well served with loungers and parasols and with all necessary facilities to hand. The main shopping is along the old road.

THINGS TO SEE & DO
Megaron Nirou ★
The excavated remains of a Minoan house. ⓐ Located just on the outskirts of Kokkini Hani, on the Iraklion side ⓒ Open Tues–Sun 08.30–15.00, closed Mon ⓘ Admission free

Water City ★★★
The biggest and best water park on the island. Speed down one of 21 slides, drift along Lazy River, beat the waves or just enjoy a swim in one of the swimming pools or the wave pool. Full range of snack-bar and restaurant facilities. See your representative for details. ⓐ Inland from Kokkini Hani along the Anopoli Road ⓣ 2810 781316 ⓦ www.watercity.gr ⓒ Open 10.00–18.00

Water sports ★
Windsurfing and waterskiing are available through the Themis Beach Hotel. ⓐ Eastern end of the beach ⓣ 2810 761412

 If there is a group of you, it might be worth trying to bargain with the water sports companies operating on the beach.

BEACHES
The Themis Beach Hotel at the eastern end of the resort, has cornered the biggest and most sheltered stretch of golden sand, but it is open to the public and has plenty of facilities, including a children's play area.

🔺 *Kokkini Hani's pleasant strip of beach*

RESTAURANTS

🍴 **Elotia Taverna** € Good, average-priced taverna with a full range of Greek dishes. Pretty, covered restaurant with a blackboard menu full of the most popular dishes and specials.
ⓐ Located on the road down to Themis Beach Hotel ⓣ 2810 762451
🕒 Open 11.00–late

🍴 **Hatzis Taverna** €€ In the village centre, this old-established taverna and apartments has tables attractively laid out around a fountain. Come here to appreciate good local cooking.
ⓣ 2810 761251 ⓦ www.hatzis-apartments-taverna.gr
ⓘ Visa and Mastercard accepted

🍴 **Themis Beach Taverna** €€ Greek and international dishes are on offer from this well-located taverna, which is associated with the Themis Beach Hotel. ⓐ Eastern end of the beach
ⓣ 2810 761412

Gouves
relaxing holiday base

Small but developing, the peaceful resort of Gouves (sometimes called Kato Gouves) lies seaward of the main Iraklion road and is a great place for winding down. There are narrow stretches of beach running the length of the resort. These are broken up into bays, with plenty of choice when it comes to shopping or eating out. Gouves also makes a good base for exploring the other resorts and sights of the northern coast.

THINGS TO SEE & DO
Water sports ★
All types of water sports are on offer on Marina beach. ➌ Marina Watersports Centre ➊ 69447 48668 ➐ Open daily

BEACHES
Good sand and sheltered conditions are to be found close to the two ports of Aphrodite, to the east, and Marina, to the west. The large beach within the former US Air Force Base, at the west end of the resort, is also open to the public.

 If you want really deserted beaches, the far west end of the resort has several small bays. They are a little pebbly but very peaceful.

RESTAURANTS
These restaurants are all on the main street leading to the beach.

Asteria € Very lively, popular taverna, with plenty of good food and drink. 'Greek' nights several times a week offer boisterous Cretan entertainment with music and dance from your warm, exuberant host, Spyros. ➌ Next door to Lavris Bungalow-Hotel ➊ Cards accepted

➎ *Gouves is a small but developing resort*

Atlantis €€ Fresh-looking restaurant decked out in white tablecloths and large umbrellas, serving a good selection of Greek dishes and fresh fish. ⓐ On the main street ⓣ 28970 42366 ⓛ Open 11.00–late ⓘ Visa and MasterCard accepted

Blue Sky Taverna €€ Special Greek menu: try the 'Greek plate' for an interesting experience! Tables scattered over a covered courtyard decked with flowers. ⓐ On the main street ⓣ 28970 41868 ⓛ Open 11.00–23.30 ⓘ Visa and MasterCard accepted

Café Totem Music Bar € Enjoy a snack and the latest chart music. A long bar and wooden tables are sheltered underneath a roof covered in vines. ⓐ On the main street ⓛ Open 19.30–late

Eliotia Taverna € This popular place offers a mixed menu including good pizzas and Greek favourites such as grilled meats. ⓐ On the main street ⓣ 28970 42820 ⓔ elotia40@hotmail.com ⓛ Open 10.00–02.00 ⓘ Cards accepted

RESORTS

Hersonissos
cosmopolitan resort

Once a small fishing village, Hersonissos is now a complex and
cosmopolitan resort. The main road drives right through the middle,
but a new bypass has diverted most of the traffic. The rocky coastline
hides sandy coves big enough to allow a full range of water sports.
Inland lie three old villages ripe for exploration: old Hersonissos,
Koutouloufari and Piskopiano.

● *Hersonissos is busy and bustling*

A thriving port from Classical Greek times, Hersonissos now trades in tourism and is busier than ever. A long linear development, it packs most activities into the space between the main road and the beach. Serious shoppers head for the main road and dice with mopeds, scooters and a constant flow of traffic to buy gold or decorated pottery. Quieter shopping is found in the side streets.

Like the resort itself, the sandy beaches are narrow and occasionally interrupted by rocky outcrops. A near-solid line of bars, tavernas and souvenir shops crowds the seafront, adding to the busy atmosphere of this resort. The beach road bustles even more in the evening and this is the place to sample a cocktail or cool beer before or after taking dinner at one of the many eating places.

Pottery, leather goods and souvenirs are often marked up in this resort, so this is an opportunity to try your hand at bartering before you decide to buy. It usually works.

THINGS TO SEE & DO
Aqua Splash ★★
Giant slides, black holes, hydrotubes and swimming pools provide watery action all day long for adults, while children enjoy their own mini-versions. Plenty of facilities in the way of fast food, restaurants and bars. Visit either for the full day or pay a reduced amount for the half day (after 14.30 hours). ⓐ Located on the Kasteli Road ⓘ 28970 24950 ⓦ www.aquasplash.com ⓛ Open 10.00–18.30 or 19.00

Boat trips ★★
There are a number of companies offering trips to Sissi and Dia. These depart once a day from the harbour.

Crete Golf Club ★★
Crete's first golf club is an impressive 18-hole park with great views and excellent facilities, including a bar, restaurant and shop. ⓐ East side of town ⓘ 28970 26000 ⓔ info@crete-golf.gr

Horse riding ★★★

Ⓐ On the main road, next door to Kartland ☎ 28970 23555

Inland villages ★★

Not far inland lies another world. The old villages of Hersonissos, Koutouloufari and Piskopiano offer a glimpse at a more traditional way of life, although they are adapting to tourism. It is a steady, uphill walk to the villages, so you should allow about 30 minutes for this. It is practical to visit the the villages all in one loop, and there are plenty of pit-stops for refreshments or a full meal – consider strolling out to one for a special dinner.

Kartland ★★

Have a go at go-karting, but check that you're covered by your holiday insurance! Ⓐ Main road, next to Star Beach Water Park ☎ 28970 25090

Star Beach Water Park ★★

The park fringes the beach, where there is a full range of water sports available, plus five-a-side football, scuba diving and even body painting. Bear in mind that it is usually full with young people and the music can be very loud. Children are well catered for here, and have their own pool and play area. There is also a first-aid centre, as well as restaurants and snack bars on hand. Moreover, should you need to contact the 'real' world, there are even facilities to send off an email. Ⓐ Main road, eastern end ☎ 28970 24472 🕐 Open 09.00–dusk Ⓦ www.starbeach.gr ⓘ Entrance free of charge to grounds, car park and swimming pools; charge for sun-loungers, parasols and most other facilities

Train ride ★★

A train departs from outside Carera Travel on the main road. It takes visitors on a pleasant one-hour journey around the town and into the old villages to the north.

EXCURSION

Anissaras ★★

Situated just to the west of Hersonissos, Anissaras is an exclusive resort, packed with upmarket hotels and apartments. This does not mean that you cannot visit the numerous excellent beaches with which this coastline is blessed.

This is also a good area for water sports. Rental equipment and lessons are available from the beachside hut near the Royal Mare hotel, at **Club Intersport** (❶ 28970 25025, ext 2950 🕐 Open 10.00–18.00 ✉ info@sun-watersports.gr).

Diving in Crete is also beginning to be explored. The **Coral Diving Centre** (❶ 28970 23282 🕐 Open 09.00–18.00), a recognized PADI centre, offers a range of dives, suitable for the complete beginner or open-water advanced divers. All equipment can be rented. Follow the signs once you get into Anissaras.

RESTAURANTS (see map on page 52)

🍴 **Hard Rock Café** €€ ❶ You can expect the usual range of burgers and steaks to be served at this well-known establishment. In addition, it attracts a lively drinking crowd in the evenings, the majority of whom come to listen to the live music. ❷ Main road ❶ 28970 24737 🕐 Open 09.00–late

🍴 **Myrtios** €€ ❷ A trip to Old Hersonissos is the perfect antidote to the pace of life in the bustling main town. Myrtios is one of many restaurants that surround the peaceful square. There is no shortage of things to choose from, and it is possible to feast on the excellent selection of starters available alone. Even the pizza is a good bet. All the food is made by hand and cooked in a traditional wood-burning oven. Traditional Greek dancing takes place in the square every Monday and Thursday in high season. ❷ Main square, Old Hersonissos ❶ 28970 24761 🕐 Open 10.30–midnight ❶ All credit cards accepted

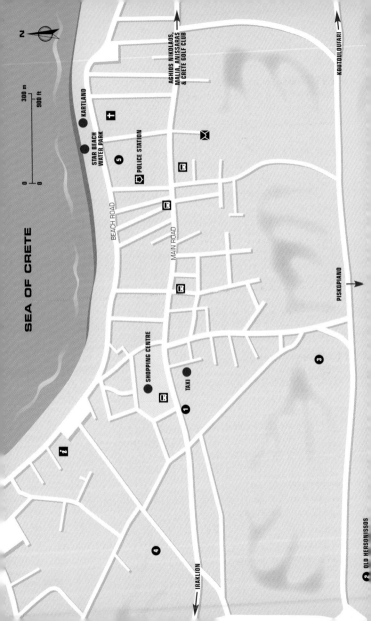

Taverna Fegari €€ ❸ Even the owner agrees that the service here is very slow. It is, but the food is good and as long as you do not mind the wait, you will have a memorable meal here, served by the friendliest Greek around. Far away from the noise and confusion in town, you will find this place a 10-minute walk from the main road, on the way to Piskopiano village. Try the Fegari special – a boned leg of lamb pan-fried and cooked with wine and fresh vegetables. The house wine is decanted from two huge wooden barrels sitting next to the till. ❸ A little out of town on the Piskopiano road ❶ 28970 24624 ❶ Open 18.00–late

Taverna Traditional Food € ❹ Not a very catchy name for a restaurant, but this is a no-frills, inexpensive establishment in a quiet part of town. The food is kept in large pots on the counter and choosing is a question of pointing at whatever you fancy. Chicken and lamb is also available from under the grill. Good chips are served here. They do cook to order, but mainly fish. ❸ West side of town ❶ 28970 24758 ❶ Open noon–very late

Vesuvios €€ ❺ This is a peaceful, relaxing restaurant in a narrow alley off the main road. It serves mostly Italian food, which seems to suit its customers, many of whom comprise those who have got bored with Greek food by the end of their holiday. The wine list is excellent, with a choice of over 40 Greek and Italian wines. The restaurant is covered in flowers and vines. ❸ Situated in the alley opposite IT After Dark nightclub ❶ 28970 21474 ❶ Open 18.00–late ❶ Visa and MasterCard accepted

NIGHTLIFE

Hersonnissos really heats up at night. There are many bars and nightclubs (some think too many) and competition is fierce to attract passers-by. Happy hour goes on all night in some bars. The partying does not stop until the sun is rising. Popular places are **New York Club**, **Camelot**, **Aira** and **Bio-Bio**.

Stalis
golden sands and water sports

Quieter than neighbouring Malia or Hersonissos, relaxing Stalis (Stalida on some maps) is a family-orientated resort that has developed beside a fine stretch of golden sands. Nothing is lacking in the way of facilities and there is a wide choice of tavernas and shops. It offers more in the way of water sports than many larger resorts.

This purpose-built resort has adopted the ancient name of Stalis, disregarding the modern name of Stalida, which is used on maps and in literature. It is a relatively small but developing resort sandwiched between the main Iraklion road and the sea. Life revolves largely around the beach by day and in the tavernas and bars by night. The road behind the beach offers the best opportunity for some gentle retail therapy, whether shopping for basic groceries or for some exotic pieces of jewellery. Shops in Stalis are generally open all day long.

    Walking eastwards along the beach from Stalis very quickly leads you into the busier resort of Malia (see page 58) offering a much wider range of services. For real peace and quiet and plenty of beach to your-self, head westwards along the beach until the beach road runs out.

THINGS TO SEE & DO
Lychnostatis Open-Air Museum ★
This unusual museum aims to give an insight into typical Cretan life, displaying a traditional furnished house, a restored windmill, a classic white church and a shepherd's shelter. You can finish off with a drink at the bar: try *kanellada* (cinnamon) or *soumada* (almond). ❸ The museum is located on the Stalis side of Hersonissos ☎ 28970 23660 ⓦ www.lychnostatis.gr ⓛ Open 09.30–14.00, closed Mon ⓘ Small admission charge

---

▶ *By day, Stalis life revolves largely around the beach*

⏣ *Stalis caters for the energetic and the not-so-energetic*

Water sports ⭑

Hang in the air, charge around at high speed or lazily paddle a tiny corner of the Aegean Sea. Whatever your choice, it is all available from one of the three water sports operators on the beach (but do not forget to check whether your holiday insurance covers you for these activities).

Skyride and **Seawolf** offer a full range of water sports activities, including waterskiing, pedalos and canoes, while **Zervas** offers slightly less but is price competitive.

BEACH

With acres of golden sand on hand, it is not difficult to find space on the beach. Facilities are good, with sun-loungers, parasols and beach showers all available. Families in particular love this beach, where you can always find room to build a sandcastle or two.

RESTAURANTS

Capricciosa € An extensive menu, from Greek to Italian, and a good menu for children. Generous portions ensure that many guests return. Good takeaway service. 🄐 Beach road ❶ 28970 31602 🕒 Open 10.00–late ❶ Visa and MasterCard accepted

George's Chicken House € Simple restaurant whose whole menu, unsurprisingly, revolves around chicken. 🄐 Beach road ❶ 28970 31213 🕒 Open 09.00–late ❶ Visa, MasterCard and Amex accepted

Hellas Taverna € Greek restaurants do not get much more traditional than this. Very friendly staff, with good food, Greek dancing twice a week, which includes loads of plate smashing, and a free glass of *raki* at the end of the meal. Anyone who comes to Stalis must come here at least once. 🄐 On the main street ❶ 28970 33820 🕒 Open from 10.00 to whenever the raki runs out

Mythos Restaurant €€ This is considered one of the best eateries on the Stalis beach road. Service is very friendly and efficient, with an extensive menu including pizzas, pasta dishes, mixed grills and a range of Greek favourites. Choose a table on the beach and watch the sunset while you eat. 🄐 Beach road 🕒 Open all day until late

NIGHTLIFE

Zervas is a lively cocktail bar which draws the under-30s (🕒 Open 18.30–late). You could also try **The Royal Oak**, a typical English bar, or **The Irish House** and **Dwyers**. Most of these you will find on the beach road.

Stalis by night is hardly a rave scene, although there is a choice of bars. Malia, on the other hand, throbs by night and is close enough to get there and back economically by taxi.

Malia
nightlife capital

Busy, hectic, lively, noisy Malia is a resort for all occasions, especially for those who live life 24 hours a day. Families might prefer the peace and quiet found away from the centre, still close enough to enjoy all the facilities of the resort, including the magnificent beaches. The adjacent old village provides a touch of traditional atmosphere.

Seaward of the main Iraklion road lies the modern resort where all activities are focused. As you stroll down the road towards the beach, past the shops, fast-food outlets and bars, the resort seems lively enough by day – but it really only comes to life after sundown. Then it throbs the night away to the beat of loud music from the various bars and, because all that dancing is bound to make you peckish, the fast-food joints stay open all night. Inland from here lies the old village, offering a very different atmosphere. This is the home of the more traditional tavernas, which are tucked away in its maze of twisting, winding streets.

THINGS TO SEE & DO
Live Greek music ★ ★ ★
Head for one of the tavernas in the square in Malia old town to enjoy a meal to the sound of live Greek music. Aim to be there for about 19.30 hours to be sure of a table.

Malia Palace ★ ★
On the outskirts of Malia lies a remarkable and extensive Minoan Palace. In many ways it is more evocative than Knossos, since little or no reconstruction has been attempted. What you see is what the Minoans left behind. Many of the finds are in the Iraklion museum. There is good information on site, and plenty to see – including archaeologists at work, since excavations are still continuing. Everything can be seen from walkways. The latest discoveries are being made in a canopied area west of the main site, as archaeologists uncover remains of a

⬆ *Ancient ruins mix with modern resorts in Crete*

considerable town that surrounded the palace. At the moment they are focusing on what appears to have been a group of large houses. ❸ Walk or cycle out from Malia along the road by the beach – the site lies just beyond Tropical Beach ⏰ Tues–Sun 08.30–15.00 ❶ Small admission charge

Water sports ★

Sea Waves Sports, on the main Malia beach, offers waterskiing, pedalos and more.

BEACHES

Malia is not short of sand, and there are huge beaches stretching away eastwards. Those looking for well-organized facilities, with bars immediately to hand, should head for the main central section, but quieter stretches of beach are found by walking out eastwards to Tropical Beach, where you can escape the crowds and the music. Families might prefer to use the beach facilities at the Sun Beach Hotel, which has a small children's play area.

Make sure the sea close by is free of rocks before renting your spot on the beach. Prices for chairs and umbrellas vary very little, but check the quality of the beach furniture, particularly the space between beds, and the availability of showers.

RESTAURANTS (see map opposite)

There are eating places to suit all tastes and pockets in Malia. Head into the old village for relatively traditional eating in a quieter atmosphere, and the resort for variety and more competitive prices.

 Delight of India €€ ❶ This is one of a rare breed of good, authentic Indian restaurants in Crete. The meals are set and there is an à la carte menu. ⓐ Malia resort ❶ 28970 33836 🕓 Open 18.00–late ❶ Visa, MasterCard and American Express accepted

The set meals, including drinks, advertised outside some restaurants offer good value for money.

Kalesma €€ ❷ No main dishes, only *mezedes*, typical Greek titbits like Spanish *tapas*. Five to six dishes for two people should be about right. ⓐ Omirou 8, Malia old town ❶ 28970 33125 🕓 Open 11.00– midnight ❶ All cards accepted

The Red Lion € ❸ Little England in a bar. Everything is English, the food, the beer, the television, even some of the waitresses. All-day breakfast and a good Sunday roast. ⓐ Beach Road, Malia resort ❶ 28970 33803. Open 09.30–late. ❶ All cards accepted.

Taverna Ilotas €€ ❹ Enjoy dining in the roof-garden of this restaurant, which is located in a quiet part of the old town. Varied menu, including grilled chicken, moussaka and peppered steak. ⓐ Aghios Yiannis Square, Malia old town ❶ 28970 33257 🕓 Open 18.00–late ❶ Visa and MasterCard accepted

MEDITERRANEAN SEA

N

| 0 | | 500m |
| 0 | | 900ft |

— STALIS

Malia Port

PYRGOS

TROPICAL BEACH, SUN BEACH →

COASTAL ROAD

BEACH ROAD

DISUSED WINDMILLS

BANANA PLANTATIONS

DOCTOR

NIK GRAMMATKI ST

DENTIST

BANK

TAXI

MAIN ROAD

AGHIOS NIKOLAOS, MALIA PALACE →

BANK

HAIRDRESSER

BAKERY

BAKERY

OLD TOWN

NIGHTLIFE

The two main nightclubs are **Apollo** ❺ and **Zoo** ❻, both on Beach Road.

Mean Fiddler ❼   Irish bar popular with people in their 20s and 30s, offering music with an Irish flavour. ⓐ Beach Road, Malia resort

Mid Way Dancing Bar ❽   Offers a large dance floor and loud music to entertain the young and nearly young. ⓐ Beach Road, Malia resort

Sportsmans ❾   Sing along with the karaoke or dance to some great party music; good and lively atmosphere. ⓐ Beach Road, Malia resort

Aghios Nikolaos
home of the 'bottomless lake'

The lake, and the life that edges it, is the big attraction of this picturesque town lying in the Gulf of Mirabello.

The capital of the Lasithi province, 'Ag Nik', as tourists like to call it, is an easy-going paradise for those wishing to relax. Little now remains of its past – there are no traces of the ancient city of Lato Etera or the fact that the Venetians built a fortress here. Tourism discovered this town in the 1960s and since then the harbour has attracted an international audience.

The lake is joined to the sea by a narrow canal; views from the hill overlooking this are quite breathtaking. The high cliffs, lush green vegetation, colourful fishing boats and tranquil restaurants make the lake an ideal place to come either at night or during the day.

A British naval traveller named Spratt measured the depth of the lake and discovered that it was over 64 m (200 ft) deep. This led him to believe that it was the opening of a deep river, and this is most probably the reason why it has become known as the 'bottomless lake'. In 1867 a man named Costas Adosidis Passas was responsible for the canal that links the lake to the sea, helping to keep the blue waters crystal clear.

 For the best views over the lake, head for the lane that leads up to the top of the town.

THINGS TO SEE & DO
Archaeological Museum ★★
A bit of a walk out of town, this is a modern, well-thought-out attraction with some interesting artefacts. It has pre- and early Minoan finds and an impressive vase in the shape of the Goddess of Mirtos. There is also an assortment of painted clay coffins and bathtubs and the grinning skull of a Roman, his forehead encircled with gold olive leaves. ⓐ On 74 Paleologou, heading out of the city towards Elounda ① 28410 24943 🕓 Open 08.30–15.00, closed Mon ❶ Small admission charge

Boat trips ★★★

Boats leave twice a day, at 10.00 and 12.30, from the harbour for the island of Spinalonga; both return at 16.30 (half-price children's fare). You may prefer to catch a boat to Spinalonga from Elounda, since these depart every half-hour. The tourist information office has details.

Folk Museum ★

This has a small but interesting collection of handicrafts, costumes and everyday Cretan artefacts. ❷ Opposite bridge and across from tourist office ❶ Open 13.30–15.00, closed Sat ❶ Small admission charge

Mini-Golf ★★

All the family will enjoy this place. As well as golf it offers table tennis, a children's pool, playground, restaurants and bars. ❸ Opposite the Municipal beach club to the south of town ❶ Open all day from 09.00 ❶ Admission charge

BEACHES

There are numerous beaches surrounding the port. The closest are Ammos and Kitroplatia, which are not particularly stunning but worth a few hours' sunbathing. Both have good facilities. A little further south, but worth the trip, is Almyros, an aquatic national reserve due to its unusual vegetation of cane bullrushes, tall trees and rare species of bird. A cool spring trickles into the sea. The beach is well organized and the water is shallow, ideal for families. More beaches lie to the north of the town, some immaculate and surrounded by upmarket hotels with private pools.

EXCURSIONS

Chapel of Aghios Nikolaos ★★

Aghios Nikolaos was named after this charming little Byzantine chapel, built in the 7th century on the spot called 'Nissi'. It is brimming with ancient frescos. From here there are also good views of the town and the bay of Mirabello. The church is not always open so you may have to get the key from the nearby Minos Palace Hotel. Drive north of the town, follow the signs off the coast road to the right, heading towards the sea.

Kritsa ★★

This is a pretty village only 9 km (6 miles) from Aghios Nikolaos. Shopaholics will want to head straight up the steep road into the main street to be tempted by the display of woven and hand-embroidered crafts. There are many Byzantine churches with wonderful frescos in the town. The most remarkable is the Panaghia Kera, with its dome and steep sides surrounded by cypress trees.

RESTAURANTS (see map opposite)

Cretan Stars €€€ ❶ Beautiful restaurant situated in the port. Dining is inside a secretive courtyard dotted with large pine trees. ⓐ 8 Akti Iosef Koundourou, almost opposite the tourist office ❶ 28410 25517 🕒 Open evenings only

Kastellos €€ ❷ Opposite the main square in Kritsa is this pleasant restaurant with a large menu. Two flights of stairs lead up to dining with a view. The speciality is steamed local rabbit with onions plus many other local dishes. ⓐ Kritsa ❶ 28410 51254 🕒 Open 09.00–late ❗ Visa and MasterCard accepted

Pelagos €€ ❸ This popular fish restaurant is well worth the short walk north around the harbour. It is an elegant place with the most evocative courtyard, filled with fruit and olive trees. ⓐ 10 Strat. Koraka and Fafouti, just behind the tourist office ❶ 28410 25737 🕒 Open 12.00–late ❗ Credit cards accepted

Taverna Aovas € ❹ Set back slightly from the road and pleasantly decorated, this is a good place to go for traditional Greek food. Try the stuffed vine leaves, rabbit *stifado* or *pasticcio*. ⓐ 44 Paleologou – same road as the Archaeological Museum ❶ 28410 23231 🕒 Open 10.00–late ❗ No credit cards

Twins € ❺ Great for a quick snack. ⓐ 17 Akti Iosef Koundourou
📞 28410 22611 🕐 Open 08.00–late ❶ All credit cards accepted

SHOPPING

Aghios Nikolaos has some of Crete's best shopping, with
quality boutiques in the streets that run up from the harbour –
Odós 28 Octóbriou, Odós Roussou Koundourou and Odós
Stakiaraki. Look out for antique and modern jewellery, embroi-
dered Cretan blouses and waistcoats, and contemporary crafts.

Paleohora
out-of-the-way gem

Once a Venetian castle, Paleohora is now a pretty village perched on the far south-west of the island. The quiet main avenue is lined with eucalyptus trees, underneath which are a few bars and tavernas. On either side of this road are two beaches: to the west, a long stretch of sandy beach and to the east, a pebbly coastline ideal for snorkelling.

The entire town is hemmed in with towering rugged mountains, giving a feeling that you are locked into another world. It is not a busy resort, being such a long drive from anywhere, but the main Venizelos Street does wake up in the evening as the atmospheric bars, restaurants and discos come alive.

THINGS TO SEE & DO
There isn't a great deal to do in Paleohora. Exploring the village, having a long lunch and sunbathing on one of the two bays is more than enough for most visitors.

Boat trips ★★
There are several companies that will sell you trips to nearby coastal villages such as Elafonissi and Sougia, and dolphin spotting early evening.

Fort ★
To the south of the harbour you can climb up some stairs to the fort. There is not much up here apart from the old walls of the castle of Selinos, built by the Venetians in 1279. The hike is worth it for the views over the peninsula.

Ferry tickets are one-way only, so you will need to buy a return ticket at your destination. Local tickets offices tend not to open until 15 minutes before the boat arrives. Ferry timetables and destinations can be found on: www.sfakia-crete.com

---

Mountain biking ★

This part of Crete is an undiscovered area for mountain biking, and a few companies in the town will rent out bikes, including **Notos Travel** (ⓐ Venizelos Street ❶ 28230 42110 ⓔ notosgr@yahoo.gr).

EXCURSIONS
Elafonissi ★★

There is a well-known walk to the west of Paleohora, along a path that follows the coastline all the way to Elafonissi. This small town boasts a tropical lagoon and beautiful sandy beaches. Elafonissi is actually an island but the waters to it are shallow and it is only a short wade across the sandbar. Buses and boats make daily journeys to the town. If you have the energy, the walk is lovely, and takes 2–3 hours. You can always arrange a boat to take you back. Avoid going at the weekend if at all possible as Elafonissi is very popular with Chaniots escaping the heat of the city, and it can get crowded.

Sougia ★

This is another worthwhile trip, again along the coastline but this time to the east of Paleohora. Sougia is a small village that has not yet attracted mass tourism. There are many simple restaurants and bars here around a huge bay of the cleanest, clearest waters you will find anywhere in the world. There is a nudist community at the eastern end known locally as the 'Bay of Pigs'.

BEACHES

The best beach is to the west and this is simply called the **Sandy Beach**. It is wide and equipped with every facility. It is well known for its high winds, and windsurfers gather from all over the island to take advantage of the conditions. There is a windsurfing rental area on the beach but it can only be used by members who pay an annual fee.

The **eastern beach** is more pebbly and not as pretty as the opposite bay, but this is where you will find the harbour and the busy promenade lined with restaurants.

RESTAURANTS

Dionysos € Well established and above average, this town centre taverna serves a good range of traditional meat and vegetable Cretan dishes. Ⓐ Venizelos St ❶ 28230 41243 ❶ Cards accepted

Oriental Bay Restaurant € This good seafood restaurant, under the shade of a pleasant terrace with views out to the sea, is at the northern end of the pebbly beach. The specials board is recommended. ❶ 28230 41322 ❶ Open 08.00–late ❶ Cash only

Pizzaria Niki € A popular pizza restaurant, also serving Greek dishes. Situated near the Sandy Beach, it is set in a lovely courtyard with trees and flowers and has more than enough room for tourists and locals. ❶ 28230 41532 ❶ Open 11.00–late ❶ Visa and MasterCard accepted

The Third Eye € A vegetarian restaurant is unusual in Greece, let alone in such an out-of-the-way community as Paleohora. It may have something to do with the fact that the town was once a hippie hangout. It still attracts environmentally conscious backpackers, who seem to flock to the town and this restaurant for its famous Greek, Asian and European vegetarian dishes. Ⓐ Situated in an unnamed street near the Sandy Beach ❶ 28230 41234 ❸ info@TheThirdEye-Paleohora.com ❶ Open 08.00–15.30 and 17.30–23.30 ❶ Cards accepted

🔽 *Paleohora's Sandy Beach*

The Samaria Gorge
adventurous walking

A National Park since 1962, the Samaria Gorge is one of the great natural wonders of Europe. Thousands of visitors walk it every year. This is not done without some toil, but the sense of achievement and satisfaction is immeasurable. For those not wishing to walk the full length, an easier option allows access as far as the great 'Iron Gates'.

The Samaria Gorge usually opens for walkers in May, once the river has subsided sufficiently to allow for safe walking; it closes in October, at the approach of the rainy season. Precise dates depend on weather conditions. Starting high on the Omalos Plain, at an altitude of around 1220 m (4000 ft), the walk is 18 km (11 miles) in length. Most of this is downhill, only levelling out at the approach to Aghia Rouméli, at the coast. Allow between five and seven hours for the walk, depending on the conditions.

The gorge is a National Park and rules do apply: no camping, no fires, no smoking, no alcohol and certainly no interfering with the wildlife and fauna. If you respect these rules you will have no problems with the helpful wardens that patrol the park.

TRANSPORT

Although it is possible to do this walk using taxis, an organized trip is the best option, especially since an experienced guide accompanies the tour (ask your representative for details). Transport is laid on (with a very early start) to take you to the start of the gorge. Breakfast can be taken either at Omalos village or at Xyloskalo, the hamlet at the entrance to the gorge. The walk ends at Aghia Rouméli on the Libyan Sea. From there, a ferry transports walkers along the coast to Hora Sfakion, where coaches await you for the return journey.

◀ *Walking the Samaria Gorge*

PREPARATIONS

Walking the Samaria Gorge is not something that can be undertaken lightly. Downhill it may be, but it can still be very tiring. Sensible preparations and precautions can do much to ensure a successful day.

Footwear Sensible shoes are key. Good, strong trainers are required, at the very least; walking shoes or boots are much preferred. Be warned – walkers with inadequate footwear may not be allowed to enter.

Sun protection Not all of the gorge enjoys shade, so it is important to guard against the sun and keep suncream handy. A hat is essential.

Water It is important to carry a bottle of water – at least a litre per person. There are springs for drinking water at various stages down the gorge. The last water in the gorge is just before entering the narrowest section. There are toilets and rest stations at various points.

Your guide Route finding is no problem – the path is easily followed. The function of the guide is to keep an eye on the party. Usually, the guide takes a longer breakfast and gives his party a head start. Following behind means that help can be offered to anyone lagging behind or in any difficulty. Guides can also summon the rescue services, if necessary.

THINGS TO SEE & DO
Xyloskalo – the head of the gorge ★★★
Wooden steps, from which the name of the hamlet of Xyloskalo is derived, lead down from the entrance into the gorge itself. Pine trees provide some shade on this steep and steady descent, and the rock face of Gingilos provides a dramatic alpine backdrop. Eventually, towards the bottom of the gorge, the path joins the Tarraios river, which runs through the gorge to the sea at Aghia Rouméli. Although it is usually dry at the higher end of the gorge, lower down the river flows for most of the summer.

Samaria Village ★★

The old village of Samaria is met roughly halfway through. Its remaining inhabitants were moved out when the area was declared a National Park in 1962. It makes a good resting place, and is where most walkers stop for a picnic. Wild goats, *kri-kri*, still survive within the gorge, and it is not unusual to see them in and around the old village.

The Iron Gates ★★★

The scenery around here rarely lacks drama but, from here on down, the gorge steadily closes in until there is only room for the river, with the cliffs rising vertically above. This spot is called Sideroportes (Iron Gates), and it is hard to imagine a more fitting climax to this spectacular walk.

Aghia Rouméli ★★

Refreshments are available immediately on passing out through the exit station, and Aghia Rouméli is just 2 km (1 mile) away. After the dryness of the gorge, Aghia Rouméli seems an absolute oasis, with tavernas, shops and accommodation. There is a small beach for a refreshing paddle or swim after the walk.

THE LAZY WAY

In this option, visitors are taken by coach to Hora Sfakion and by ferry to Aghia Rouméli. A 2 km (1 mile) walk, slightly uphill, leads to the entrance of the gorge. A further walk soon leads to the narrowest and most spectacular part of the gorge. The lazy way it might be, but this is no soft option. The route is fully exposed to the sun, and forms the hottest part of the walk. Water must be carried and sensible footwear is essential.

Gortys, Faistos & Aghia Triada

It is worth hiring a car to drive south, through ever-changing country-side, to visit some of the most important archaeological sites on Crete. Starting from Malia, this 215 km (135 mile) tour takes in the Roman city of Gortina, now called Gortys, whose remains lie scattered among olive trees, plus the Minoan palaces of Faistos and Aghia Triada, sitting in the tranquil mountains. There is the opportunity to have lunch or relax on the beach at Matala (see page 32) , or even stay for one of its reputedly fantastic sunsets.

All these sites can just as easily be reached from Rethymnon, along the Spili to Mires road. From Malia, head along the new National Road to Iraklion. Take the third Iraklion exit (first if you are coming from Rethymnon) – signposted Mires – and head south via Agii Deka. Look for the site entrance to the right on reaching Gortys.

Gortys ★★★

The remains of this one-time capital of Roman Crete lie scattered over a large area, among the surrounding olive groves and on the hillside above the site. A café and display of statues are found to the right of the pay kiosk, and the entry charge gives access to the fenced-off area around the Church of Aghios Titos. St Titos was sent by St Paul to convert Crete to Christianity and became the first Bishop of Crete. Also in this enclosure is the Roman agora (marketplace), an odeon (small theatre) and a 10 m (33 ft) long wall on which the Laws of Gortina are written in Ancient Greek. ● Open 08.00–18.00 ❶ Admission charge

Faistos ★★★

Continue to Mires, and look for the signposted left turn to Faistos. Set on a hilltop, the **Minoan palace of Faistos** provides a marvellous panorama over the surrounding countryside. Smaller than Knossos, but in many ways similar to it, this palace was rebuilt after earthquake damage. Most of what is seen now is the New Palace, the older part

🔺 *Some of the many remains of Roman Crete at Gortys*

being to the left of the site entrance. This older part is where the original Minoan town once spread down to the plain below.

🕐 Open 08.00–19.00 ❗ Admission charge

Aghia Triada ★★★

To reach Aghia Triada, continue past the car park and take the right-forking road almost immediately. This elevated road offers superb views over the plain as it winds along the hillside for 3 km (2 miles) until the surfaced road ends at the car park. The Minoan villa and small town lie in a wonderful pastoral setting overlooking the Mesara Gulf.

In Minoan times, the plain below was probably covered by the sea, which would have lapped the base of the hill. This evocative site was once thought to have been an extension to the palace at Faistos, used as a summer residence and known as the Royal Villa. Later finds and the existence of a small town cast doubts on that purpose, suggesting either a cult association or a central gathering point for celebrations.
🕐 Open 08.00–15.00 ❶ Admission charge

Matala ★★
Return to the junction near Faistos and turn right down to the main road where another right turn leads to Matala (see page 33). Here you will find a sandy beach backed by tamarisk trees fronting the azure-blue sea, offset by creamy yellow cliffs honeycombed with 2nd-century AD rock-cut tombs. The beach is rimmed by tavernas built to make the most of the views, and a bazaar-like shopping alley (with a well-stocked bookshop) runs parallel to the beach. Return to Malia via Agii Deka and Iraklion.

🔽 *Matala and its rock-cut tombs*

Knossos

**Knossos offers a fascinating backward glance over 4000 years,
to the earliest known organized civilization in the Mediterranean.
Not only does Knossos qualify as one of the world's most important
archaeological sites, but it is also one of the most visited. Most of
the vast treasures and finds from the site are housed in Iraklion's
Archaeological Museum (see page 38).**

The site of ancient Knossos is located some 5 km (3 miles) from the
centre of Iraklion. ❶ 2810 231940/226092 ⏰ Open 08.00–19.00
(summer); 08.00–17.00 (winter) ❶ Admission charge

The services of a guide are a big advantage for first-time visitors
to the site. This means taking advantage of an organized trip
(ask your representative for details). Private visitors are often pestered
by unofficial guides, who expect payment.

BACKGROUND

Evidence suggests that the earliest settlement on this site was neolithic
(from around 6000 BC). The Minoans arrived around 3500 BC, bringing
skills in bronze working, and they survived until around 1100 BC. Their
civilization is often divided into Early, Middle and Late periods, and these
too are usually subdivided. Interest really starts in the Middle Minoan
period, around 2000 BC, when the first palaces were built, encouraging
a more centralized society. These early palaces were destroyed by
earthquakes around 1700 BC (marking the start of the Late Minoan
period) but they were rebuilt in a more elaborate style. It is the remains
of these last palaces that are visible today.

DISCOVERY

Arthur Evans began digging at Knossos in 1900, and was soon making
spectacular finds that astonished the whole of Europe. Without the
scientific backing of present-day knowledge, Evans' interpretation and

theories were on the whole remarkably accurate, although many are challenged in detail today. The biggest criticism concerns his reconstruction of palace rooms and frescos. Ownership of the site passed to the British School in Athens in 1924 and to the Greek Government in 1952.

MYTH OF THE MINOTAUR

The complex underground network of corridors and rooms in this Minoan palace gave rise to the myth of the Minotaur. According to legend, this bull-headed monster was kept in a labyrinth and fed on human flesh.

THINGS TO SEE & DO

Site tour ★★

There is much to see and understand in this ancient palace. The following account concentrates on the main features and is, by necessity, brief.

West Court This is the first part reached from the entrance. It is crossed by partly restored raised walks. Notice here three large pits which are thought to have been repositories for offertory oil, wine and sacrificial animals. The court runs up to the West Facade, which is faced with gypsum blocks, now badly weathered. Quarried locally, the gypsum cladding made the palace appear gleaming white. Following around to the right leads to the West Porch. On the right here are excavated remains of later houses.

Corridor of the Procession Fresco From the porch, wooden doors opened to this corridor. The walls on both sides were lined with huge frescos showing figures in procession. Landslip has destroyed much of the corridor.

South Propylea This paved area is especially visited to see a copy of the Cup Bearer Fresco, one of the best-preserved parts of the fresco from the corridor. Red supporting columns were used in the reconstruction. These were once wooden, often whole trees with the thicker ends uppermost.

🔺 *Knossos: 4000 years of history*

◗ *One of the reconstructed frescos at Knossos*

From here a staircase leads to the main reception rooms. Storerooms full of *pithoi* (giant storage jars) – used for grain, oil and wine – are still in place and can be seen from the upper long corridor. Reproductions of some of the most famous frescos lie in this area.

Central Court This large, open space gives access to the throne room on the right. Remarkably, the original gypsum throne, in the inner sanctum, now some 3500 years old, survives intact.

Royal Apartments These lie on the opposite side of the central court and include the Grand Staircase, the Queen's Megaron (central hall), complete with bathroom, and the Hall of the Double Axes (the King's Megaron).

The Charging Bull Leaving the central court by the north entrance brings you face to face with the relief of the charging bull, the original of which is now in the museum in Iraklion.

Iraklion Archaeological Museum ★
Organized trips usually combine Knossos with a trip to the museum in Iraklion (see page 38), where many of the finds are housed. It's hard not to marvel at the skill of the artisans throughout the Minoan period.

The Lasithi Plateau

With its white-sailed windmills, the Lasithi Plateau is one of the abiding images of Crete. There are not so many windmills today, but this fertile plateau still rumbles on with a donkey-driven rural lifestyle. Tourists provide a new outlet for the traditional handicrafts, lace and woven carpets, which often decorate the roadsides. This full-day tour is around 120 km (75 miles).

From Malia head towards Iraklion and shortly turn into the road sign-posted to Mochos and the Lasithi Plateau. Follow the road as it winds upwards to 800 m (2600 ft) and dramatically arrives at the Lasithi Plateau through a cutting lined with the relics of stone windmills once used for grinding grain.

 Watch out for the coaches that bully their way up and down these mountains. They drive quite fast and take up more of the road than they should.

The Lasithi Plateau, a patchwork of green fields, flanked by the stark slopes of the Dikti mountains, is extremely fertile and grows a wide range of vegetables, grain and fruit, though frequent winter snow makes it unsuitable for olives or citrus crops. The white-sailed windpumps are a product of 15th-century Venetian engineering. There were 10,000 windmills at one time. Far fewer operate now, although many of their skeletons still stand. A windmill in full sail these days usually signifies a taverna.

Turn right at the first junction to pass through Kato Metochi and Plati, with its tempting displays of craftwork hung along the street. Turn right on entering Psikro.

THINGS TO SEE & DO
The Diktean Cave ★★
According to legend, this cave is the birthplace of the god Zeus. His father, Kronos, fearing that a son would usurp his power, had sworn

to eat any male offspring. Rea, the wife of Kronos, tricked her husband by giving him a stone to eat while leaving Zeus hidden in this cave. The baby was protected by the Kouretes, who beat their shields outside to disguise the baby's cries. Follow the road flanked by carpets to reach the car park. You can hire a donkey (at great expense) to ride up to the cave entrance, or climb steadily through 105 m (350 ft) to the top. On entering the moderately illuminated cave, steps lead deep down into

⬤ *One of the many windmills in the Lasithi Plateau*

the interior. A short circuit around the bottom gives views of the stalactites and stalagmites. The game now is to spot the stone nipples where young Zeus was suckled. 🕐 Open 09.30–16.00 ❶ Admission charge

> The smooth steps leading up to the Diktean cave are very slippery, so make sure you wear proper footwear. It can get quite cold, so take a jumper or warm top.

Cretan Folklore Museum ★

Pretty villages follow in succession as the tour around the plateau continues. Aghios Georgios is worth a stop for its folklore museum. Located in a typical village house, it gives an insight into the old Cretan way of life. Furnished rooms, tools, costumes and farming implements are all well displayed in a series of rooms. 🕐 Open 10.00–17.00 ❶ Small admission charge

Just a little higher up is the folklore museum dedicated to Eleftherios Venizelos, one of Crete's most famous statesmen. ❶ Admission free

There are one or two working windmills to see on the last part of the drive around the plateau, as well as the largest town, Tzermiado. This is the last chance to buy a carpet or lacework before leaving the plateau. Leave the plateau once you have passed through Pinakiano.

A BITE TO EAT

Kali Mera € This pretty restaurant, 1.5 km (less than a mile) before the village of Psikro, is a great spot for lunch. It has inspiring views over the plateau with the huge mountain range in the background framing the landscape. The restaurant is covered in flowers. The food is simple and very Greek. ❸ Aghios Charalampos ☎ 28440 31913 🕐 Open 07.00–late ❶ Visa and MasterCard accepted

Santorini
jewel of the Greek islands

Unique among Greek islands, Santorini is the stuff of picture postcards, a visual experience not to be missed. Colour-splashed houses nestle tightly on dark, volcanic hillsides to create memorable images. Optional tours of the island allow visitors to see more than just the capital. Altogether it makes for a long – but satisfying – day out. In fact, a day is not long enough for most visitors. Despite it's being expensive, people are now choosing to spend their entire holiday, or at least part of it, on the island.

Explosive volcanic activity here, particularly around 1450 BC, is believed by some to have contributed to the decline of the Minoan civilization on Crete, creating such upheavals that land around sank, leaving this once circular island in fragments. Santorini is the name of the largest of the islands left in the aftermath.

GETTING THERE

Day cruises are on offer from Iraklion, Rethymnon and Aghios Nikolaos. Large cruise ships are used, offering a good level of comfort – which is very necessary, since some eight hours of the day will be spent aboard.

> Not all ships offer the same onboard facilities. Some have swimming pools, for example. See your representative for booking details, and ask about facilities before booking.

THE CRUISE

Depending on the departure port, boarding takes place at around 06.30 Breakfast is taken on board, as is evening dinner on return, and the cost is normally included in the ticket. At some stage in the morning there is a short presentation, giving brief details of Santorini and outlining the optional tours on offer. These tours can only be booked on board the ship.

OPTIONAL TOURS

Ancient Akrotiri The first stop is Pyrgos before the coach moves on to the ancient Minoan city of Akrotiri. Plenty of time remains to explore the capital Fira on the return.

A beach day at Pyrgos Again, the first port of call before heading off to the black sands at Kamari (see page 91).

Hot springs and volcanoes A small boat sails out to two of the islets within the group to explore the hot springs on Palea Kameni and then the sulphurous volcano on Nea Kameni.

Round the island tour This visits Pyrgos (see page 88) and Oia (pronounced 'Eea'; see page 92) before returning to the capital Fira. Oia is the longest stop, allowing time for lunch to be taken in one of the many tavernas.

These tours only take place if there is sufficient support. Only after bookings have been made are decisions taken, but refunds are given or there is the chance to transfer in the event of a cancellation.

DISEMBARKING

The cruise ships arrive at around 11.30. The ship docks first at Athinios to allow those passengers to leave who are going on trips. Unlike Fira, Athinios is at sea level with road access for coaches. Those staying on board are taken on to Fira, where disembarkation is by tender to the shore. Fira (also spelt Thira) is perched 260 m (850 ft) above and is reached by cable car, donkey or on foot. All passengers are given a ticket when leaving the ship, valid for the cable car or donkeys.

BEACHES

Because of its volcanic history, Santorini is renowned for its many coloured beaches. You can choose from secluded areas to the more cosmopolitan, with watersports and a range of facilities. The main beaches are:

● *Kamari's black sand beach is popular among tourists*

Akrotiri This is the famous red beach of the island near the Church of Aghios Nikolaos.

Avis This can be found in between the resorts of Kamari and Monolithos and is very good for watersports.

Kamari A large, well-known beach with all the facilities you could ever want or need.

Monolithos A popular beach with shallow waters.

Oia The port of Armeni, below the town of Oia, has many small areas for swimming and sunbathing. Close by are also the beaches of Baxedes and Kouloumbos.

Perivolos This is the longest beach on the island, stretching from Perissa village to Perivolos. It is possibly also the most popular because of its many tavernas, bars and various watersports.

Vlichada Right down on the southernmost point of the island, this beach is unique because of its sand dunes, which have often been likened to a lunar landscape.

> **KAMARI TOURS** For a wide selection of tours of the island
> you could not find a better company. ⓐ GR-84 700 Kamari
> ① 22860 31390 ⓕ 02860 31497 ⓦ www.kamaritours.gr

AKROTIRI

The prehistoric settlement of Akrotiri is at the southern end of the
island. The ruins date from the Late Bronze Age (1650–1500 BC) and
establish beyond doubt that a well-developed Minoan-type civilization
existed on the island. The destruction of such a civilization here, by the
eruption of the Thera volcano, which submerged much of the island
under the waves, often raises questions about whether this is the
mythical lost city of Atlantis.

The layering of buildings one on top of the other suggests that this
site could have been a very early form of today's block of flats. The wall
paintings here are the earliest example of large-scale painting in Europe.

The city is under cover to protect it from the weather, but walkways
have been set up inside so that visitors can get close to the buildings.
ⓐ Akrotiri Archaeological Museum ① 22860 81366 ⓛ Open 08.30–15.00,
closed Mon ❶ Small admission charge; no flash photography

PYRGOS

All roads lead to the old capital, Pyrgos, or so it seems. This fortified town
sprang up in the Middle Ages and looks more attractive from afar. There
is not much to do here except walk up to the highest point for the views.
There are cafés and snack bars around for those not choosing to walk.

SANTO WINE TOUR

There are 850 vine growers on the island, harvesting 2540 hectares
(6276 acres) of land. They have formed a cooperative with Santo Wines,
one of the largest producers on the island, situated to the west of
Pyrgos. Visitors can take in a tour of the modern plant and sample
a few of their excellent vintages. ① 22860 25128/22596
ⓦ www.santowine.gr ⓛ Open 09.00–21.00 ❶ There is a small
charge for the tour with wine-sampling

HISTORY OF WINE-MAKING ON THE ISLAND

Wine-making in Santorini goes back over 3500 years, when it is thought that wine was not only produced but also exported from the island.

Santorini's unique climate of very hot, dry conditions and harsh winds means that the growers have had to invent a way of training and pruning the vines that they call *koulooura* (curl). The vines are pruned into the shape of a basket and, for their protection, the grapes are placed in the centre. The night mists provide moisture for the vine, and the volcanic earth the variety of minerals that help the grapes to flourish.

Of the well-known wines, the Nikteri and Vinsanto are the most famous. The latter is a sweet red wine made from grapes that have been dried in the sun for 10 to 15 days.

⬤ *The hilltop town of Pyrgos*

FIRA (THIRA)

Situated around the hilltop on several terraces, Fira boasts white houses, pretty churches, narrow streets, cafés, restaurants, fast-food outlets and the inevitable tourist shops. Bargain hunters can spend their day haggling for gold, silver or an onyx chess set.

The best things are free, however, and that includes the magnificent views from the cliffs. The cable car leaves from the northern end of town. Near here, too, is the island's archaeological museum.

THINGS TO SEE & DO

Archaeological Museum ★

Good examples of early Cycladic figurines from Akrotiri and Mesa Vouna. ● Open 08.00–14.30, closed Mon and public holidays ❶ Small admission charge

---

 Bargain hard in the shops, as competition is fierce for your business! Fira has plenty of shops among its many lanes.

RESTAURANTS

Kastro € A simple cafeteria serving sandwiches and snacks only but with fantastic panoramic views. ❸ Directly opposite the cable car ❶ 22860 22503 ● Open noon–15.00 and 18.00–late ❶ All major credit cards accepted

Koukoumaulos €€€ If you need pampering or just want to spoil yourself then come here. Behind the large blue doors you will find chic international cuisine in the prettiest courtyard decked out in Mexican style. ❸ At the far southern end of town ● Open 18.00–late ❶ All credit cards accepted

Nicolas €€ Traditional Greek cuisine with a blackboard menu that changes every day. The menu is in Greek but the owners will happily translate everything for you. ❶ 22860 24550 ● Open noon–15.00 and 18.00–late

KAMARI

Kamari is how a modern resort should be built. Everything is tidy while retaining a feel of old Greece.

THINGS TO SEE & DO

Cinema ★★★

The outdoor cinema on the outskirts of Kamari is a must. It is such a pleasant experience seeing a film under the stars that it does not really matter what you are watching! Food and drink can be bought from the bar at the back, before the film or at the half-time interval. A truly unmissable experience.

Mountain biking ★

Lava Trails Hire out good-quality bikes for half- or full-day trips. ❶ 22860 31165 Ⓦ www.motorinn.gr (with downloadable map) 🕒 The shop is open 08.00–22.00; tours are 08.00–14.30 once or twice a week

Water sports ★

Sadly, the main beach in Kamari is currently not very well equipped for water sports, but there are plans in hand to change that. Ask around.

Volcano Scuba Diving Offer a range of dives around the island. ⓐ In Kamari town ❶ 22860 33177 Ⓦ www.scubagreece.com 🕒 Open 09.00–21.00 ❶ Visa card accepted

RESTAURANTS

Atmosphere €€€ Fine international cuisine in stylish surroundings within earshot of waves crashing on the beach. ⓐ Beach promenade, above Kamari Tours ❶ 22860 31368 🕒 Open 18.00–late ❶ Visa and MasterCard accepted

Dimitris Place € This is a cheap, no-frills restaurant on the outskirts of town offering excellent Greek food. ❶ 22860 32748 🕒 Open 09.00–late

OIA

Located in the north of the island, the fishing village of Oia (pronounced 'Eea') was severely damaged by an earthquake in 1956 but has been rebuilt in traditional Cycladic style. With its clustered white houses, tiny courtyards, colourful churches and narrow streets, it competes strongly for the title of prettiest village on the island.

Oia is also the place where artists gather, their work inspired by the magnificent surroundings here. It is also the best place on the island to watch the sun setting into the sea.

THINGS TO SEE & DO

Armeni ★★

This small traditional port is at the foot of Oia. It is possible to drive down but it is much more rewarding to use the steep, winding steps. There are a few tavernas here, but most people make the trip for a refreshing swim in the clear water.

 The best things in life are free, and nothing will beat watching the sun set in Oia.

RESTAURANTS

 1800 Restaurant €€€ First-class restaurant in a first-class setting. Few places will beat this place for style and the quality of food. Bit expensive for what is basically simple Mediterranean food. ⓐ On the main street ⓣ 22860 71485 ⓕ 22860 71800 ⓦ www.1800.gr ⓛ Open 19.30–03.00 ⓘ All credit cards accepted

 **Minims €** This coffee shop serves the most fantastic cakes and coffee and has one of the best views out across the sea towards the two volcanic islands. ⓐ You cannot miss it on the main street

 **Thalami €€** This fine restaurant specializes in typical dishes from Santorini. ⓐ On the main street ⓣ 22860 71009 ⓛ Open 12.00–late ⓘ All credit cards accepted

Food & drink

GREEK DELIGHTS

Greek cooking uses the freshest ingredients and is nourishing, tasty and filling. As there are also a large number of vegetable dishes; this is a cuisine ideally suited to vegetarians (ask for *horis kreas* – without meat). So, although in every resort you will be sure to come across English standards – like bacon and eggs, chips, shepherd's pie and roast beef and Yorkshire pudding – do not miss out on what the Greeks have to offer.

CRETAN DISHES

Venture into a traditional taverna away from tourist areas and you will find a whole range of Cretan specialities, such as *staka*, melted cheese mopped up with bread, or *dakos*, rusk-type bread sprinkled with olive oil, cheese and tomato. Part of the fun is to try something different. Fried snails in a vinegar, tomato and herb sauce are especially delicious.

Appetizers

A typical Greek meal begins with a basket of fresh bread and a selection of *mezedes* (appetizers). Order several dishes and share them with your friends. Served hot or cold, the highlights are: *horiátiki*, a refreshing salad comprising feta cheese, tomato, cucumber and black olives; *tzatziki* – cucumber and yoghurt dip; *taramasalata* – a paste of cod roe and lemon juice; and *saganaki* – fried cheese fritter. Cheese or spinach pies also make tasty snacks.

Main courses

Meat is cheap and plentiful. The most succulent dishes include: *souvlaki* or *shish kebab* – garlic-marinated lamb dressed with onions; *keftedes* – meatballs with mint, onion and eggs; *moussaka* – layers of minced lamb with sliced aubergine and bechamel sauce; and *stifado* – beef with onions and tomato sauce. Or you might like to try *dolmades* – vine-leaf parcels stuffed with rice, minced beef or pork and pine kernels and braised in lemon and olive oil.

🔺 *Saláta horiátiki, a refreshing salad shown here with wine and bread*

Fishermen's catches of red mullet, sole, snapper or sea bream may be brought to your table if you have found a seaside taverna that takes your fancy. Before ordering it is important to remember that fish is sold by weight; negotiate a price first – a good rule of thumb is that 1 kg (2 lb) serves four people.

Prawns, stuffed mussels, fried squid and stewed octopus (often cooked in white wine, with potatoes and tomatoes) are all widely available. Swordfish steaks are popular, but expensive. *Soupia* (cuttlefish) on the barbecue, is excellent.

If you suddenly become peckish around lunchtime but do not want to sit down to a full meal, *gyros* – doner kebab in pitta bread – or the snack version of *souvlaki* – pitta bread filled with meat, tomato and onion – will fill a hole.

Desserts

Most Greeks will settle for fresh fruit after a meal – watermelons are unbelievably juicy, or there are apricots, peaches and grapes. If you have a sweet tooth, try *baklava*, a pastry soaked in honey with almonds and walnuts, *loukoumades*, a kind of honey fritter, or *bougatsa*, a hot pie with a creamy filling of custard and cinnamon. More revitalizing on a hot day is yoghurt topped with honey and almonds – delicious!

DRINKS

Soft drinks, like Cokes and lemonades, are sold everywhere, but freshly made orange or lemon juice is more refreshing in hot weather. Mineral water (still or fizzy) is equally thirst-quenching – Greek brands are perfectly safe and acceptable. Outside the hotels, tea generally means hot water and a tea bag!

Greek coffee is served in small cups, is strong in flavour, has a treacly texture and leaves a thick sediment. Ask for *gliko* if you like it sweet, *metrio* (medium), or *sketo* (without sugar). If you prefer you can order espresso or instant (ask for *Nes*). And there is nothing more refreshing on a hot day than iced coffee (*frappé*), usually served in a glass and available in packet form (add water!) in supermarkets.

Spirits

The Greek national drink is *ouzo*, an aniseed-flavoured spirit usually taken as an aperitif. Ouzo can be drunk straight, but if you intend to have more than one glass, follow custom and dilute it with water and ice. You may also be offered *raki*, a spirit made from distilled grape skins and pips. Greek brandy is also highly palatable, and available in various strengths

THE KAFENEION

In Cretan villages, the *kafeneion* (café) remains very much a male preserve, although visitors of both sexes will be made welcome. Locals come here to read the paper, debate the issues of the day and play *tavli* (backgammon), as well as to consume *café ellenico* (Greek coffee). This is made by boiling finely ground beans in a special pot with a long handle. Sugar is added during the preparation rather than at the table, so you should order *glyko* (sweet), *metrio* (medium) or *sketo* (no sugar). It is never mixed with milk. In summer, try *frappé* (with ice).

and prices, indicated by star ratings (3, 5, 7). The best-known brand of Greek brandy is Metaxa, which is dark and sweet, but you could alternatively ask for the drier Kamba.

Wine & Beer

The most distinctive Greek wine is *retsina*. Flavoured with resin, it takes some getting used to and you may prefer to drink it with soda water. *Retsina* is a good accompaniment to white fish and is supposed to complement the oil in Greek food.

Crete produces some excellent wines. The island is covered in vineyards and the locals are rightly proud of what they regard as some of the best wines in Greece. There are four main vine-growing areas on the island: Peza, Sitia, Arhanes and Dafnes. Arhanes is thought by some to be the same vineyards that the ancient Minoans cultivated, almost 4000 years ago.

Greek lager is very drinkable and can be cheaper than imported beer – ask for Mythos or Hellas. The most widely available foreign brands are Heineken, Amstel, Henninger and Budweiser. Specify that you want a bottled or draught beer, as cans are often poor value.

Menu decoder

Here are some of the authentically Greek dishes that you might encounter in tavernas or pastry shops.

dolmadákia vine leaves stuffed with rice, onions, parsley, mint and lemon juice

domátes/piperiés yemistés tomatoes/peppers stuffed with herb-flavoured rice (and sometimes minced pork or beef)

fassólia saláta white beans (haricot, butter beans) dressed with olive oil, lemon juice, parsley, onions, olives and tomato

lazánia sto fourno Greek lasagne, similar to Italian lasagne, but often including additional ingredients, such as chopped boiled egg or sliced, Greek-style sausages

makaronópita pie made from macaroni blended with beaten eggs, cheese and milk, baked in puff pastry

melitzanópita pie made from baked liquidized aubergines mixed with onions, garlic, breadcrumbs, eggs, mint and Parmesan cheese

melitzanosaláta aubergine dip made from baked aubergines, liquidized with tomatoes, onions and lemon juice

moussakás moussaka, made from fried slices of aubergines, inter-layered with minced beef and béchamel sauce

píta me kymá meat pie made from minced lamb and eggs, flavoured with onions and cinnamon and baked in filo pastry

pastítsio layers of macaroni, haloumi cheese and minced meat (cooked with onions, tomatoes and basil), topped with béchamel sauce and baked

saláta horiátiki country salad (known in Britain as 'Greek salad'); every restaurant has its own recipe for this salad, but the basic ingredients comprise tomatoes, cucumber, onions, green peppers, black olives, oregano and feta cheese dressed with vinegar, olive oil and even more oregano

🔺 *Stuffed vine leaves (dolmadákia) and olives*

souvláki kebab – usually of pork, cooked over charcoal

spanakotyropitákia cigar-shaped pies made from feta cheese, eggs, spinach, onions and nutmeg in filo pastry

taramosaláta cod's roe dip made from pureed potatoes, smoked cod's roe, oil, lemon juice and onion

tyropitákia small, triangular cheese pies made from feta cheese and eggs in filo pastry

tzatzíki grated cucumber and garlic in a dressing of yoghurt, olive oil and vinegar

Shopping

CARPETS AND RUGS

Basic woven mats and rugs can be found everywhere at reasonable prices. Better-quality carpets are also available, but be sure to check their authenticity.

DELICATESSEN CHOICES

The pungent smell of herbs and spices usually announces an Aladdin's cave of local gourmet delights. Honey and intriguing jams such as fig, tangerine and carrot with honey, jars of cherries and other fruit preserved in sugar syrup, an assortment of nuts, cheeses and *raki*, the local heady tipple, even sponges, all jostle for shelf space.

⬤ *A colourful array of Cretan delicacies*

JEWELLERY

Gold and silver jewellery shops abound with an extensive range of designs. The quality of the jewellery is generally excellent and most gold items are 14 carat. Silver jewellery is particularly good value. Prices of jewellery are unlikely to be displayed, as vendors are not keen on potential customers making comparisons with rivals. Despite this, prices tend to be similar.

LACE AND EMBROIDERY

The choices here are limitless, with bedspreads, tablecloths, mats and clothing available in traditional designs and colours. Displays are particularly enticing in country villages. where the women sit outside working at their craft.

LEATHER

Leather is one of the island's specialities. Leather Alley, in Chania, has a huge choice of belts, handbags, sandals, satchels and Cretan-style boots but there are many other leather outlets around the island.

MUSEUM REPLICAS

Many replicas of items on display in Greek museums are on sale in tourist shops, but most are cheap and crude. It is worth paying extra for the excellent reproductions available from recognized museum shops, such as the Loggia, at Rethymnon, and the shops to be found close to the archaeological museum entrance in Iraklion.

OLIVE-WOOD CARVINGS

Olive wood is particularly beautiful to look at and handle. Check out the wood carvers in Anopoli, and Nikos Sirgas, at 2 Petalioti, in Rethymnon (see page 22).

POTTERY

A wide range of Cretan pottery is available, from basic traditional wine and oil jars to more sophisticated designs and finishes.

Children

Greeks love children, so having them around presents little problem. The danger is that you will be ignored in favour of them. In summer especially, Greek families tend to stay up until after midnight. They congregate in the local square, which is usually closed to traffic after 18.00, for a meal or drink at around 22.00. This makes it safe for children to run around with their friends, while parents relax.

BOAT TRIPS
Children love being on the water, so play pirates for a day by sailing to a remote beach with a picnic, either on an organized trip or by hiring your own boat. Sailing trips can also include some sightseeing, watching fish through a glass-bottomed boat, searching for dolphins or fishing. Your holiday representative will have full details of all the options.

CASTLES AND RUINS
Ancient sites and castles with reasonably unrestricted access are Lato, the Minoan palace at Malia, Frangokastelo Castle, Rethymnon Castle and the fort at Iraklion. Keep a close eye on your children, however, as not all dangerous areas are fenced off or protected.

STAR BEACH WATER PARK
Something for everyone at this water park in Hersonissos (see page 50). Entrance is free to the grounds, car park and swimming pools but everything else has to be paid for. The park is very close to the beach, where you will find all kinds of watersports. Children have their own play area while the adults can amuse themselves with paragliding, bungee jumping and water slides. There are restaurants and snack bars plus the chance to email back home. ❸ Hersonissos, main road eastern end ❶ 28970 24472/24434 Ⓦ www.starbeach.gr ❺ mail@starbeach.gr ❶ Open April–Oct, 08.00–dusk

---

❶ *Children love being by the water*

WATER CITY

Crete's biggest and best water park (see page 44). Ask your holiday representative for details. ⓐ Just inland from Kokkini Hani
ⓣ 2810 781 316/355 ⓦ www.watercity.gr ⓛ Open daily 10.00–18.00

WATER SPORTS

In the main tourist areas there is no shortage of watersports activities for children, such as pedalos and canoes. A flag system is in operation on most beaches, and there is usually a guard on duty on all the more popular beaches.

Sports & activities

GO-KARTING
Hersonissos Kartland Behind Star Beach Water Park. ☎ 28970 25090
Rethymnon Kart Club With a 600 m (656 yd) track. ☎ 28310 23398

GUIDED WALKS
The Happy Walker Rethymnon ☎ 28310 52920 ⓦ www.happywalker.com
Trekking Plan Aghia Marina/Platanias ☎ 28210 60861 ⓦ www.cycling.gr

The best walking books available on the island are *Landscapes of Western Crete* and *Landscapes of Eastern Crete*, published by Sunflower Books.

HORSE RIDING
Melanouri Horse Farm Lessons for both beginners and the more advanced. From Moonlight rides to trekking through picturesque olive groves and forgotten villages. Food is provided. ⓐ Near Matala ☎ 28920 45040 ⓦ www.melanouri.com
Horse and wagon Tours Karteros (near Iraklion). Trekking, riding lessons, organic farm holidays. Cooperates with Therapeutic Holidays Camp. ☎ 2810 380244 ⓦ www.ride2crete.com

MOUNTAIN BIKING
Paleochora Notos Mountain Bike Rental. ☎ 28230 42110.
Santorini Island Lava Trails, Kamari. ☎ 22860 31165. ⓦ www.motorinn.gr

SAILING
Chania Venetian harbour, Evangelos glass-bottomed boat.
Hersonissos M/S Calypso, Dia Island, snorkelling, BBQ.
Rethymnon Venetian harbour, Dolphin Cruises, Pirate Ship and Popeye Ship. ☎ 28310 57666. ⓦ www.crete-web.gr/cruises/captain hook

SCUBA DIVING

Anissaras Coral Diving Centre ☎ 28970 23282
Chania Blue Adventures Diving ☎ 28210 40608.
Ⓦ www.blueadventuresdiving.gr
Elounda Nikos Sub-Diving School, Elounda Beach Hotel
☎ 28410 41576
Hersonissos Nana Beach Hotel ☎ 28970 24076
Rethymnon Rithymna Beach Hotel ☎ 28310 71002

WATER SPORTS CENTRES

There is a whole range of water sport activities available all along
the island's coastline. Below are just are few places to try.
Anissaras Club Intersport ☎ 28970 25025
Chania A whole range available from operators along the shore
between Platanias and Chania.
Hersonissos A wide range of water sports on the main beach.
Kokkini Hani Club Pappilon, Thermis Beach, offers a good range
of watersports.
Rethymnon Water sports available on the main town beach, including
speedboat hire and fishing.
Stalis Opportunities for
skyride, paragliding and
water sports; Sea Wolf
Watersports also offers
full range of activities,
or try Zervas, in front
of Zervas Hotel.

TENNIS

Chania Tennis Club.
☎ 28210 44010.

▶ *Jet-skis offer fun for all*

Traditional Cretan costume

Festivals & events

Panigiria (festivals) play a large part in Greek culture, especially saints' days. Wine festivals are held around the island in the autumn and arts festivals throughout August. Check out dates and venues at the local tourist office. Papas (priests) still play a large part in the life of the community. Although younger Greeks are less inclined to religion, the Papa is still called in to bless a new car, shop and even traffic lights. Organized folk evenings are the nearest most tourists get to Greek folk culture, but some restaurants have live music and maybe some dancing.

SAINTS' DAYS

The whole of Greece would be on permanent holiday if every saint's day was celebrated but, fortunately, only major saints warrant a near shutdown. Villages often have their own saint, so it is not unusual to arrive unexpectedly in the middle of a celebration, which always starts with a church service, before the real business of feasting and dancing begins. Among the feasts that are celebrated island-wide are the following:

- **23 April** St George (celebrated on Easter Monday or Tuesday, if Orthodox Easter is late)

- **24 June** John the Baptist

- **20 July** Profitis Ilias (the Prophet Elijah – to whom most small churches on hill tops are dedicated)

- **15 August** Assumption of the Virgin – one of the biggest feasts

- **25 August** Aghios Titos in Iraklion

- **11 November** St Minas Protector, patron saint of Iraklion

LIFESTYLE

EASTER

The greatest festival in Greece is Easter, which is more important even than Christmas. Almost everything shuts down for at least three days, and it can be difficult to find a bus or taxi. The date of the Greek Orthodox Easter is moveable and only coincides with the rest of Europe every few years.

Good Friday Tolling bells and yellow candles accompany the solemn processions in the evening, parading the flower-decorated bier of the dead Christ.

Easter Saturday Evening service ends as all lights are extinguished at midnight. To the deafening sound of church bells and firecrackers, the priest lights a candle whose flame is then used to light the white candles of the congregation with the announcement *Christos anesti* (Christ has arisen).

Easter Sunday Easter is celebrated with spit-roasted lamb and raki.

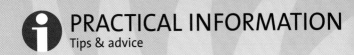

Preparing to go

GETTING THERE

The cheapest way to get to Crete is to book a package holiday with one of the leading tour operators. Those specializing in Crete offer flight-only deals or combined flight-and-accommodation packages at prices that are hard to beat by booking direct. If your travelling times are flexible, and if you can avoid the school holidays, you can also find some very inexpensive last-minute deals on the Internet.

Make sure you also check the Travel supplements of the weekend newspapers such as the *Sunday Telegraph* and the *Sunday Times*. They frequently carry advertisements for inexpensive flights, as well as classified adverts for privately owned villas and apartments available to rent in most popular holiday destinations.

BY AIR

Crete has two international airports, both renowned for delays. Chania serves the west of the island and Iraklion the centre and east. There are numerous charter companies offering flights to Crete during the summer months, although if you travel out of season, you may have to use a scheduled international flight to Athens and change terminals to take an internal flight on **Olympic Airlines**, the Greek national airline.
UK office 🅐 11 Conduit Street, London W1R oL. 🕿 0870 606 0460
🅕 020 7629 9891 🅦 www.olympicairlines.com

If you can be flexible about when you visit, you can pick up relatively inexpensive special deals. As a rule, the further in advance you buy your ticket, the cheaper it usually is – but you can also get good last-minute deals from online travel agents via the Internet.

HELLENIC TOURISM ORGANIZATION

Further information about Crete can be obtained from the
Hellenic Tourism Organization 🅐 4 Conduit Street, London W1S 2DJ
🅣 020 7495 9300 🅕 020 7287 1369 🅔 info@gnto.co.uk
🅦 www.gnto.gr

BEFORE YOU LEAVE

Holidays should be about fun and relaxation, so avoid last-minute panics and stress by making your preparations well in advance.

It is not necessary to have inoculations to travel in Europe, but you should make sure you and your family are up to date with the basics, such as tetanus. It is a good idea to pack a small first-aid kit to carry with you containing plasters, antiseptic cream, travel sickness pills, insect repellent and/or bite-relief cream, antihistamine tablets, upset stomach remedies and painkillers. Suntan lotion can be more expensive in Crete than in the UK so it is worth taking a good selection – especially of the higher factor lotions – if you have children with you. Also make sure you do not forget after-sun cream.

If you are taking prescription medicines, ensure that you take enough for the duration of your visit – you may find it impossible to obtain the same medicines in Crete. It is also worth having a dental check-up before you go, although if you do have problems with your teeth while in Crete there are many excellent dentists.

DOCUMENTS

The most important documents you will need are your tickets and your passport. Check well in advance that your passport is up to date and has at least three months left to run (six months is even better).

All children, including newborn babies, need their own passports now, unless they are already included on the passport of the person they are travelling with. It generally takes at least three weeks to process a passport renewal. This period can be longer in the run-up to the summer months. For the latest information on how to renew your passport and the processing times, contact the **Passport Agency** ☏ 0870 521 0410 ⓦ www.ukpa.gov.uk

You should check the details of your travel tickets well before your departure, ensuring that the timings and dates are correct.

If you are thinking of hiring a car while you are away, you will need to have your UK driving licence with you. If you want more than one driver for the car, the other drivers must have their licences too.

MONEY

You will need some currency before you go, especially if your flight gets you to your destination at the weekend or late in the day after the banks have closed. Traveller's cheques are the safest way to carry money because the money will be refunded if the cheques are lost or stolen. To buy traveller's cheques or exchange money at a bank you may need to give up to a week's notice, depending on the quantity of foreign currency you require. You can exchange money at the airport before you depart. You should also make sure that your credit, charge and debit cards are up to date – you do not want them to expire mid holiday – and that your credit limit is sufficient to allow you to make those holiday purchases. Do not forget, too, to check your PIN numbers in case you have not used them for a while – you may want to draw money from cash dispensers while you are away. Ring your bank or card company and they will help you out.

INSURANCE

Check that your insurance policy covers you adequately for loss of possessions and valuables, for activities you might want to try – such as scuba diving, horse-riding, or water sports – and for emergency medical and dental treatment, including flights home if required.

After January 2006, a new EHIC card replaces the E111 form to allow UK visitors access to reduced-cost, and sometimes free state-provided medical treatment in the EEA. For further information, ring EHIC enquiries line: ☏ 0845 605 0707, or visit the Department of Health website Ⓦ www.dh.gov.uk

CLIMATE

Average daytime temperatures: **April** 20°C (68°F); **May** 24°C (75°F); **June** 29°C (84°F); **July** 31°C (88°F); **August** 32°C (90°F); **September** 29°C (84°F); **October** 24°C (75°F).

You will often find that the southern coast experiences temperatures up to 10°C or 18°F higher. In spring and autumn you might need a sweater at night, especially if you want to eat outside. Crete has quite high humidity, more so in the west, which often makes it feel hotter than it is. The best dress rule to follow is to wear layers so that if you get too hot, you only need to remove a shirt or sweater.

SECURITY

Take sensible precautions to prevent your house being burgled while you are away:

- Cancel milk, newspapers and other regular deliveries so that post and milk do not pile up on the doorstep, indicating that you are away.
- Let the postman know where to leave parcels and bulky post that will not go through your letterbox – ideally with a next-door neighbour.
- If possible, arrange for a friend or neighbour to visit regularly, closing and opening curtains in the evening and morning, and switching lights on and off to give the impression that the house is occupied.
- Consider buying electrical timing devices that will switch lights and radios on and off, again to give the impression that there is someone in the house.
- Let Neighbourhood Watch representatives know that you will be away so that they can keep an eye on your home.
- If you have a burglar alarm, make sure that it is serviced and working properly and is switched on when you leave (you may find that your insurance policy requires this). Ensure that a neighbour is able to gain access to the alarm to turn it off if it is set off accidentally.
- If you are leaving cars unattended, put them in a garage, if possible, and leave a key with a neighbour in case the alarm goes off.

AIRPORT PARKING AND ACCOMMODATION

If you intend to leave your car in an airport car park while you are away or stay the night at an airport hotel before or after your flight, you should book well ahead to take advantage of discounts or cheap off-airport parking. Airport accommodation gets booked up several weeks in advance, especially during the height of the holiday season. Check whether the hotel offers free parking for the duration of the holiday – often the savings made on parking costs can significantly reduce the accommodation price.

PACKING TIPS

Baggage allowances vary according to the airline, destination and the class of travel, but 20 kg (44 lb) per person is the norm for luggage that is carried in the hold (it usually tells you what the weight limit is on your ticket). You are also allowed one item of cabin baggage weighing no more than 5 kg (11 lb) and measuring 46 by 30 by 23 cm (18 by 12 by 9 in). In addition, you can usually carry your airport purchases, umbrella, handbag, coat, camera, etc., as hand baggage. Large items – surfboards, golf-clubs, collapsible wheelchairs and pushchairs – are usually charged as extras, and it is a good idea to let the airline know in advance if you want to bring these.

CHECK-IN, PASSPORT CONTROL AND CUSTOMS

First-time travellers can often find airport security intimidating, but it is all very easy really.

- Check-in desks usually open two or three hours before a flight is due to depart. Arrive early for the best choice of seats.
- Look for your flight number on the TV monitors in the check-in area, and find the relevant check-in desk. Your tickets will be checked and your luggage taken. Take your boarding card and go to the departure gate. Here your hand luggage will be X-rayed and your passport checked.
- In the departure area, you can shop and relax, but watch the monitors that tell you when to board – usually about 30 minutes before take-off. Go to the departure gate shown on the monitor and follow the instructions given to you by the airline staff.

TELEPHONING CRETE

To call Crete from the UK, dial 00 30 followed by the ten-digit number

During your stay

AIRPORTS

Both airports on Crete are well served by reasonably good roads, but if you are driving yourself you should always allow plenty of time to reach your airport when flying back.

BEACHES

In summer, many beaches have lifeguards and a flag safety system. Other beaches may be safe for swimming but there are unlikely to be lifeguards or life-saving amenities available. Bear in mind that the strong winds that develop in the hotter months can quickly change safe beach into a not-so-safe one, and some, such as Falassarna and Georgióupoli, can have strong currents the further out that you go. If in doubt, ask your local representative or at your hotel.

CONSULATE

British Consulate in Crete ⓐ 16 Odós Papalexándrou, (third floor) Iraklion ⓣ 2810 224012 ⓔ crete@british-consulate.gr

CURRENCY

In line with the majority of EU member states, Greece entered the single currency on 1 January 2002. Euro (€) note denominations are 500, 200, 100, 50, 20, 10 and 5. Coins are 1 and 2 euros and 1, 2, 5, 10, 20 and 50 céntimos (also called Lepta).

Although the drachma has now been replaced by the euro, you will find many shops and tavernas display prices in both currencies, which can be quite confusing because often the euro sign, if badly written or printed, looks remarkably like the pound sign. Check the exchange rate before you travel to Crete – unlike the drachma, the euro is more stable. Changing money: banks are found in main towns but are absent from some of the smaller resorts. They open at 08.00–14.00 on Monday to Thursday and 08.00– 13.30 on Friday. In high summer, many open

between 17.30 and 20.15 on weekday evenings. Exchange bureaus are found in all tourist resorts. Cash machines taking major bank cards and Eurocheque cards are increasing in numbers.

 The highest exchange rate is only a good deal if the rate of commission charged is not excessive.

CUSTOMS

Cretans are renowned for their *filóxenia* (hospitality to strangers) and you are bound to experience it in one way or another during your stay. If you are invited to eat or drink with a Cretan it is considered insulting if you try to pay your share; you can always try to reciprocate with a gift at a later time (a bottle of imported whisky is considered a good present), but be warned: if you make a gift they will try to give you something in return! Especially in the hotter summer months, most Cretans take a 'siesta' between 14.00 and 17.00, one of the reasons why a lot of shops are closed during that time. Cretans rarely begin their evening meal earlier than 21.00, and usually take the whole family along, babies too. Children are generally allowed to wander around restaurants at will, even late at night. When drinking in the company of a Cretan, never fill their glass to the top – it is considered to be an insult.

DRESS CODES

If you are visiting churches or monasteries you will not be allowed in wearing shorts or beach clothes; it is best to wear long trousers or a skirt and take a shirt or wrap to cover your shoulders. If you are invited into a private home in Crete, again it is impolite to arrive in shorts – Cretans love to dress up, whether to go out or to entertain at home.

ELECTRICITY

Voltage in Crete is 220 volts, which is compatible with the UK, but you will need a 2-pin adaptor to fit Greek sockets. It is important to realize that electricity is expensive in Greece, so please be considerate in your use of it; for example, do not leave air conditioning on in your room when you go out. There may be power cuts due to excessive demands, but these rarely last long. If you are buying electrical appliances to take home, always check that they will work in the UK before you buy.

FACILITIES FOR VISITORS WITH DISABILITIES

Both Hania and Iraklion airports do have special toilets, but sadly that appears to be the extent that Crete has gone to accommodate the disabled. Overall, the island is distinctly short of amenities for visitors with disabilities, and that applies to locals as well as visitors. See if an organization for the disabled at home can advise you before you take your holiday; they will probably have information that will be of help, especially if you are travelling independently, and they may even be able to put you in touch with somebody with first-hand experience of holidaying in Crete. In general, however, you will find Cretans are considerate and helpful towards those with disabilities.

GETTING AROUND

Driving conditions Remember that in Crete you drive on the right. You do not need an international driving licence, just your normal one. Driving insurance is inclusive in your car rental, but if done locally there are two levels of insurance available, so make certain you have the fully comprehensive one. Always carry your driving licence, passport and any other relevant documents with you when driving – if stopped by the police for any reason you will be expected to produce them. It is worth noting that on roads like the National Highway (*Ethniki*), what would appear to be the hard shoulder on a European road is in fact the slow lane on Crete, used to allow faster traffic to pass. But beware of the local farmer who parks in this lane so he can water his olives! If you are stopped by the police for a motoring offence you are expected to pay your fine on the spot (make sure you get a receipt if you do). If you do not pay, the police will remove the licence plates from your car, which you will then have to reclaim from the police station on payment of the fine. If anything like this happens you should contact your hire company immediately – they will know what to do.

Car hire and driving Drivers need to be over 21 (25 in some cases) and hold a valid driving licence, which they must have with them. The cheapest is not always the best. Much depends on the quality of the car and on the back-up service. Your holiday representative can help here. Cars with air conditioning are now much more common and these can be a cheaper option than open-top 4WDs in the height of the summer. Beware of flashy drivers trying to overtake on narrow roads. The National Highway is a good wide road that runs across the top of the island linking the four main cities all the way to Kastelli. Other roads can vary in quality from straight metalled roads to unsurfaced tracks with giant potholes. Where you encounter the latter, slow down, or you could easily damage your wheel rims and end up stranded with one or more flat tyres.

Public transport The bus service is good to major towns, and particularly along the north coast. Buses are a cheap way to explore and tend to operate to the timetable, but it is best to be at the bus stop a little before a bus is due. Ⓦ www.bus-service-crete-ktel.com, for timetables

Taxi Taxis are comparatively inexpensive; do, however, be prepared for the driver to stop and take on other passengers.

HEALTH MATTERS
Medical help There are a number of private medical clinics offering a 24-hour service and with English-speaking doctors. Details available at local pharmacies or the small 'health houses' found in most resorts.

Pharmacies These often have English-speaking staff and are very helpful for minor complaints and illnesses. They operate a rota system for opening outside normal shop hours (especially at the weekend) and information about the duty chemist is displayed in each shop.

Generally both over-the-counter and prescription drugs purchased at pharmacies in Crete will be cheaper than in England. However, some, such as antibiotics, can be expensive. If you been prescribed drugs by a local doctor during your stay, due to illness or accident, you should be able to reclaim the cost through your medical insurance. Pharmacies are not like chemists shops in the UK so you are unlikely to find razor blades or soap for sale, but in major resorts most will cater for tourists by selling suntan cream, etc. Homeopathic and herbal treatments and remedies are very popular in Crete and widely available. Personal hygiene goods are to be found in most supermarkets.

Water Tap water is safe enough but no good to drink. The high mineral content can cause minor stomach upsets, so it is better to use bottled water.

Precautions Cooling breezes off the coast can mask the intensity of the sun's rays, which can burn you if deflected off sand or nearby water. You can even burn in the shade, especially if you have sensitive skin. If you drive a car with an open sun roof, keep your shoulders covered and wear a hat. The same applies if you are wandering around shopping. Keep covered up during the hottest part of the day and drink plenty of water to avoid dehydration.

Sea urchins are quite common in rocky coastal regions; if you step on one the spines can be removed with tweezers. You should then douse the affected area with lemon juice or ammonia; you can buy ammonia 'sticks', which are also good for jellyfish stings, at pharmacies.

Mosquitoes can be a nuisance but are easily dealt with by burning insect coils or using an electric deterrent. If you want to avoid the attention of wasps, bees and hornets just ensure that you do not leave food out, especially sweet or sticky food.

THE LANGUAGE
A difficult language, the beauty of Greek is that it is phonetic. Greeks love to hear visitors attempt to speak it. However, most signs are in Greek and English, and English is so widely – and well – spoken that you can happily trundle through a fortnight without needing to learn a word of Greek.

THE GREEK

Greek	Name	Pronounced
Α α	alpha	a
Β β	beta	b
Γ γ	gamma	g, but becomes y in front of e and i
Δ δ	delta	d
Ε ε	epsilon	e as in extra
Ζ ζ	zeta	z
Η η	eta	e as in eat
Θ θ	theta	th
Ι ι	iota	i
Κ κ	kappa	k
Λ λ	lamda	l
Μ μ	mi	m

Greek	Name	Pronounced
Ν ν	ni	n
Ξ ξ	xi	x
Ο ο	omicron	short o
Π π	pi	p
Ρ ρ	rho	r
Σ σ	sigma	s
Τ τ	taf	t
Υ υ	ypsilon	u
Φ φ	phi	ph
Χ χ	chi	ch as in loch
Ψ ψ	psi	ps
Ω ω	omega	long o

ENGLISH

General vocabulary

GREEK (pronunciation)

yes/no	*neh/Okhee*
please/thank you	*parakahLO/efkhareesTO*
hello/goodbye	*YAsoo/andEEo*
good morning/good afternoon/evening	*kahleeMEHRa/kahleeSPEHRa*
good night	*kahleeNEEKHtah*
OK	*enDACKsee*
excuse me/sorry	*signomee*
Help!	*Voylthia!*
today/tomorrow	*siMEHRa/AHvrio*

Useful words and phrases

open/closed	*anikTON/klisTON*
right/left	*thexia/aristerA*
How much is it?	*POso kAni?*
Where is a bank/post office?	*Poo Ine i TRApeza?/to tahithromEEo?*

ENGLISH	**GREEK** (pronunciation)
Useful words and phrases (continued)	
doctor/hospital	*YAHtros/nosokoMEEo*
police	*assteenoMEEa*
I would like...	*Tha Ithela...*
menu	*menOO*
toilets	*tooahLEHtess*
mineral water	*emfialoMENo nerO*
bread	*psomEE*
fish/meat	*psarEE/krEas*
beer/wine	*bEEra/krasEE*
Cheers!	*Steen eeyEEa soo!/YAHmas!*
coffee with milk	*kafEs (me gAla)*
Can we have the bill, please?	*Mas fErnete ton logariasmO, parakalO?*
I don't understand/	*then katalaVENo/*
Do you speak English?	*MilAteAnglikA?*

MEDIA

Even the smaller resorts now sell English newspapers, usually only a day or two out of date. Locally produced newspapers in English can be a useful source of information about local events. There are quite a few cinemas on the island, including a couple of open-air ones, and Crete has several local TV and radio stations, but none English-language.

OPENING HOURS

Shops Traditional shopping hours in Crete are 08.00–14.30 on Monday and Wednesday, 08.00–14.00 and 17.00–20.00 on Tuesday, Thursday, Friday and 08.00–13.00 on Saturday. Tourist resorts are a case apart and most shops open all day, usually from early morning until 23.00. Sunday is a general closing day, but shops serving tourism mostly remain open.

Churches are almost always open for visiting, but you often have to find the lady in black who looks after the key.

PERSONAL COMFORT AND SECURITY

Crime Most of the larger tourist resorts suffer from petty theft, often committed by other visitors. Take as much care of your personal property as you would at home. Watch out particularly for bag snatchers and pickpockets in crowded places and keep a firm hold on your camera. Theft from cars is another problem. Be sure to leave nothing on display when leaving the car and never leave anything of value in the car at any time, even locked in the boot. The use of safe deposit boxes, wherever available, is recommended. If you lose your passport or any other important document it is imperative that you report it to the police and the Consulate of Great Britain as soon as possible. Get a copy of any police report, since you may need it if you make an insurance claim.

Police The civil police keep a low profile but invariably turn up when needed, at motor accidents and crime scenes, and to deal with illegally parked cars. Parking in the narrow streets of towns and villages can be a problem. The police may show tolerance towards local inhabitants over parking, but are less inclined to treat hire cars with the same degree of leniency. There are also tourist police, who speak several languages and are trained to help with problems faced by tourists.

Public toilets Public toilets are found in bus stations and main squares. Smarter facilities are found in bars, but you should buy a drink if you are using them. Toilets are generally very clean, but you must observe the practice throughout Greece and not flush away used toilet paper. Do as the Greeks do and put it in a bin (provided in each cubicle) next to the toilet. Remember this, or you risk blocking the pipes!

Restricted areas There are many bases on Crete for the Greek army, navy and air force. These are protected rigorously, and if you see signs warning you not to take photographs please observe them. It is also worth remembering that the recent case of British plane spotters being tried for and convicted of spying was based not on photographs taken, but on information they wrote down in notebooks.

POST OFFICES

Most post offices are open Monday to Friday 08.00–14.30, the main ones in Hania and Iraklion until 19.30 and on Saturdays. During the tourist season there are also mobile post offices, big yellow caravans, which appear in places several tourist areas. They are often open on Saturdays and Sundays. Post boxes are bright yellow with a blue logo on; at major post offices you will find two slots – *esoterikó* for local mail and *exoterikó* for overseas. Outside the main towns they are not always emptied every day. Postcards can take up to two weeks to get to Britain, letters three or four days; if you want your postcards to arrive back home before you do then put them in an envelope.

RELIGION

Crete like Greece is dominated by the Greek Orthodox Church with a faith that has strong historical roots in the local community. Saints' days and name days are very important days to celebrate, and their religious overtones are quickly lost to the Cretan enthusiasm for feasting and dancing. The attitude is very much 'work hard and play hard', but the church and religion are still a very big part of everyday life, especially in the villages. Weddings, baptisms and funerals are serious and lengthy occasions.

TELEPHONES

If you have a telephone in your room, you will probably be given a bill at the end of your stay – the calls made will have been metered. You can also make calls from *periptero*, the little kiosks selling sweets, papers and cigarettes, or in smaller villages from the local *kafenion*. They will also have a metering system and you will be told how much your call costs at the end.

You will need a phone card, available from street kiosks and a wide number of shops, for most public phones. A couple of short calls to the UK will use about 100 units. Phone calls are cheaper after 22.00 and on Sundays. If you are thinking of taking your mobile phone to Crete it is advisable to check first with your supplier or subscriber to see if it will work. If you do bring one, you may find reception sparse or patchy in some regions – in low-lying areas.mountains can block the signal.

EMERGENCY NUMBERS

Ambulance 166   Police 100   Fire Brigade 199

PHONING ABROAD

To call an overseas number, dial **oo**, then the country code (UK = **44**), then the area code (minus the initial **o**), then the number.

TIME DIFFERENCES

Crete is in the same time zone as Eastern Europe, therefore 2 hours ahead of the UK. Clocks go forward 1 hour on the last Sunday in March and back 1 hour on the last Sunday in September, just as in England.

TIPPING

In restaurants a service charge of between 10 and 15 per cent will be included in your bill. However, it is accepted that a small tip will be given to the waiters – usually you will find your change contains several coins which (within reason, and only if you feel inclined to) you leave behind. It is also customary to tip taxi drivers, hotel porters, chambermaids and hairdressers. If you are shown around a church by the 'keyholder' or priest, a tip is also welcome, but to avoid embarrassment this should always be left at the entrance to the church rather than offered directly to the guide.

WEIGHTS AND MEASURES

Imperial to metric

1 inch = 2.54 centimetres
1 foot = 30 centimetres
1 mile = 1.6 kilometres
1 ounce = 28 grams
1 pound = 454 grams
1 pint = 0.6 litres
1 gallon = 4.6 litres

Metric to imperial

1 centimetre = 0.4 inches
1 metre = 3 feet, 3 inches
1 kilometre = 0.6 miles
1 gram = 0.04 ounces
1 kilogram = 2.2 pounds
1 litre = 1.8 pints